Building China

Building China

Informal Work and the New Precariat

Sarah Swider

ILR Press
an imprint of
Cornell University Press
Ithaca and London

First published 2015 by Cornell University Press

First printing, Cornell Paperbacks, 2015
Printed in the United States of America

Library of Congress Cataloging-in-Publication Data

Swider, Sarah Christine, author.
Building China : informal work and the new precariat / Sarah Swider
pages cm
Includes bibliographical references and index.
ISBN 978-0-8014-5415-8 (cloth : alk. paper)
ISBN 978-0-8014-5693-0 (pbk. : alk. paper)
1. Construction workers—China. 2. Construction industry—China.
3. Informal sector (Economics)—China. 4. Migrant labor—China.
5. Labor movement—China. I. Title.
HD9715.C62S95 2015
331—dc23

2015012131

Cornell University Press strives to use environmentally responsible suppliers and materials to the fullest extent possible in the publishing of its books. Such materials include vegetable-based, low-VOC inks and acid-free papers that are recycled, totally chlorine-free, or partly composed of nonwood fibers. For further information, visit our website at www.cornellpress.cornell.edu.

Cloth printing 10 9 8 7 6 5 4 3 2 1
Paperback printing 10 9 8 7 6 5 4 3 2 1

To my mom, Tula Grande; my daughters, Olivia and Tula;
my husband, Marcin Szczepanski; and all of the amazing
construction workers in my life.

Contents

Preface

The context of research—and the position of the researcher within that context—is of fundamental importance to any research agenda. It shapes the research question, structures how the research is conducted and situates the outcomes (Harding 1987; Behar 1996). To fully understand the research presented in this book, then, it is important to ask: How did a white woman who grew up around farmers in one of the whitest states in the United States (Vermont) come to research male construction workers in China?

My interest in the struggles of the working class began when I took a job at a local restaurant at a hotel in a college town in Vermont. I became close friends with many of the other workers in this establishment. Some were college students who worked to earn spending money, but most were primary wage earners who had been in service work as cooks, waitresses, and room cleaners for decades. These workers were called "lifers" by the college students who moved in and out of these jobs. The lifers, in turn, called the college students "flatlanders" because they often came from places like Massachusetts, whose flat landscapes contrasted to the mountains of Vermont.

In a society that disdained their jobs, the "lifers" struggled to maintain dignity through hard work. In Vermont's Yankee Puritan culture, a hard worker is a good worker. Though the lifers worked harder than the flatlanders, they also held a longer list of grievances against the bosses. At staff meetings, they repeatedly raised issues such as the lack of health insurance, the slipping hazard posed by the kitchen steps, and violations of the informal seniority system. I found myself situated in both groups and in neither. As a local I was on the path of lifer, but I was also a college student, though not a flatlander, which created opportunities for me to follow alternative life paths.

I participated in this micro-ecosystem with a mix of curiosity and confusion until one of my college instructors assigned excerpts from Marx asserting that the need to "work" and be productive is what makes us human. Marx's discussion of the social relations that create labor, the realities of alienated labor, and the exploitation of the working class helped me reflect on my work at the hotel. At around the same time, I saw my boss truly angry for the first time. Red-faced, he stormed through the building yelling and waving a small pamphlet. Two days later, one of the lifers was fired. It turned out that the pamphlet that ignited my boss's rage was a brochure from a labor union that had rented the banquet hall. Though I knew little of unions at the time, my boss's uncharacteristic anger indicated that he feared them, which convinced me that unions must be powerful. The intersection of these events—my exposure to Marx in the classroom and the experience of working and seeing the power of unions—sparked what would become a lifelong interest in labor, labor unions, and worker resistance.

Later, while interning in Washington DC, I watched Congress fast-track the North American Free Trade Agreement (NAFTA). Attempts to include provisions for worker protection failed miserably. At the same time, newspaper and magazine headlines promoted story upon story about outsourcing, manufacturing relocations, and deindustrialization. In this context, I decided to pursue a graduate education in the hope of understanding how workers could survive and maybe even thrive in this new global political economy.

Before graduate school, I headed to South Korea for a year to gain some international experience and perspective. One year turned into three (1995–98), and I experienced the vagaries of the global economy as I lived through the Asian Financial Crisis and saw its impact on my close friends. It seemed that no one was spared as people who worked in both white- and blue-collar employment across different industries lost their jobs. I witnessed firsthand the effects of forced restructuring and austerity produced by the International Monetary Fund's (IMF) Structural Adjustment Programs (SAPs). These "structural adjustments" required a set of new national laws that made it easier to fire full-time, long-term workers in favor of part-time, temporary and contracted workers. According to the IMF, these policies produced the "flexiblization" of labor necessary for Korea to restore fiscal balance and global competitiveness.

I participated in the countermovement organized by unions, which culminated in the first general strike since the Korean War. The strike brought workers across all industries out into the streets, effectively shutting down the entire country. It was in Korea that I was radicalized as I learned about unions, strikes, and the efficacy of labor protests through direct participation. During this time, I also became aware of the "awakening of the sleeping dragon" as China emerged onto the world scene. I started learning Chinese, believing that if I really wanted to understand the dynamics shaping working-class struggles across the globe, I would have to understand what was happening in China. Since my first stay in Korea, I have regularly returned to Asia, spending a total of almost a decade in East and Southeast Asia, in some cases watching firsthand as industrial capital has helped create "low-wage" workers. At the same time, I have watched, learned about, and participated in countermovements by workers resisting exploitation and shaping the ways in which they would become integrated into the global economy; as Silver and Zhang (2009) suggest, "Where capital goes, conflict follows."

Graduate studies kept me coming back to Asia as I focused on two aspects of labor movements, both of which were considered exceptions rather than the norm: cross-border labor cooperation and organizing among the "unorganizable." During this rather gloomy historical period for labor, labor advocates took hope from cases of successful organizing and political action among the weakest workers. This included organizing among migrants in the United States (Milkman and Wong 2000), self-employed women in India (Bhatt 1989), and street vendors in Mexico (Cross 1998). Others focused on cross-border labor cooperation (Gordon and Turner 2000; Frundt 1999) or global unionism (Waterman 2004; Lillie 2005) as potential ways that labor could deal with global capital.

My own research focused on a case study of domestic workers in Hong Kong who were mainly women immigrants from countries in Southeast Asia. Immigrant women working in private homes as nannies and domestic workers are considered "unorganizable" because they do not have a common employer, their workplaces are in the private realm, there is a high turnover rate, and many labor protections do not extend to domestic (and immigrant) workers. However, the women I studied had organized a domestic workers' union that was highly successful in winning protections and benefits including paid maternity leave, minimum pay increases, and severance pay. The union also provided women with legal assistance, temporary housing, and educational programs. Their amazing success provides some lessons for other precarious and vulnerable workers. Specifically, these workers may need to look beyond traditional union structures. The union for migrant women domestic workers gave each nationality equal rather than proportional representation and had a networked structure that created flexibility that allowed the union to form temporary coalitions with other organizations (Swider 2006).

Meanwhile, China's entrance into the global economy was creating a massive new army of precarious workers. China's urban workers had been protected under the "iron rice bowl" policy, which provided cradle-to-grave benefits including day care, education, health care, and retirement. Mao's workers' paradise underwent painful restructuring and privatization during the contemporary era of economic reform that began in 1978. The social compact represented by the iron rice bowl arrangements, in which workers agreed to lower wages in exchange for job stability and sustenance, was broken, and workers were thrown into the ocean to sink or swim on their own (Tang and Parish 2000).

At the same time, China embarked upon a path of urbanization that included releasing agricultural workers from the land by reforming the collectivist farming system. As a result, hundreds of thousands of farmers entered cities as "peasant workers." Many peasant workers, mostly women, entered into factories in China's growing export-oriented manufacturing sector (Pun 2005; Lee 1998). These women migrant workers, also known as *dagongmei*, played a central role in earning China the nickname, "the world's workshop." Because they make so many of the products that are consumed around the world, these workers have become highly visible both to academics and in the popular media.

One summer, I was in China studying the Chinese language and reading about how these peasant women were becoming workers as they entered the factories (Lee 1998; Pun 2005) and service economy (Hanser 2006; Otis 2007) and how contentious this process was as they organized and protested against their exploitation (Chan 2001). Every day I would sit on the roof of our building, reading and watching the construction workers across the street build a building that literally emerged over the summer. On the ground, the site was surrounded by walls, and while the building began to jut into the sky, the workers and their lives in the cities took place behind these walls and remained invisible. It was only once I discovered my "quiet" reading spot on the roof that I became cognizant of the hundreds of workers living and working on the site. One day, a few of the workers ventured down the street to buy cigarettes from a kiosk, and I tried to talk to them. However, my basic Chinese skills combined with their accents made it impossible. A Chinese friend from the university explained that they were all migrant workers from other parts of China. The following year, when I returned to China for language study, I spent my free time wandering the city looking for construction sites, which were everywhere. My Chinese had progressed to the point where I was able to talk to workers and learn about where they came from and their lives in the city. Despite the fact that there are more men migrants than women, and they are concentrated in a few industries including construction, I could not find anything written about these men who were building China. I discovered that most migrants do not end up in the factories; rather, most enter into the urban informal economy, a sector that is largely missing from the story of China's economic rise and role in the global economy. I decided to focus my research on these men migrant construction workers who had changed my image of China's growing urban economy and would change my perspective on China's emerging working class.

As a white, middle-class female graduate student from the United States studying male migrant construction workers from some of the poorest segments of China's society, I feel compelled to address positionality and power. Positionality refers to how relationships and interactions are influenced by age, gender, race, nationality, and class. In my fieldwork practice, I decided not to act as an impartial outsider or credentialed expert. Instead, I created my own space with migrant construction workers by participating actively in their daily lives. In other words, I neither became one of them, nor did I objectively record their lives. Instead, the data that constitute this book come from my experiences among them. My questions were formulated from my perspective and their answers to prior questions. I believe that because I lived, worked, and played with migrants, they had the opportunity to learn from me, and I definitely learned from them. In this sense, this research is constructed from a multitude of dialogues that occurred over time.

Despite my willingness to develop a life in China with migrant workers, I remained a white, middle-class woman from the United States; my gender, race, and nationality constantly shaped my research, though their intersecting effects varied across contexts. For example, professors and friends warned me that it would be dangerous to spend time with construction workers, especially at night. In the Chinese popular press at the time, migrant men were treated as the perpetrators of sex crimes against women. Despite these warnings, spending time with migrant men rarely scared me because I viewed the fears of migrant men as based in stereotypes rather than in real danger. In addition, my status as an American provided me with some protection because the consequences for harming a foreign national were greater than for harming another Chinese person. In other words, whereas my gender might have made me weak in the eyes of men seeking to do harm, my nationality was a protective shield. However, there were limits to this protection. For example, the more powerful and well-connected labor contractors occasionally made me feel vulnerable to harassment; as men used to getting what they wanted, they seemed not to fear repercussions from the government. In this case, I think my gender trumped my nationality. In addition, some of the men in the street labor market did not hesitate to grope or rob me. In contrast to the powerful contractors, I believe these men operated without fear because they had little to lose.

Sometimes my gender and nationality were strongly present in my interactions, and at other times they seemed to fade to the background. For example, I regularly visited some jobsites during the evenings and spent time in the dorms. When I arrived, the guard or a worker would give a warning that I was coming. By the time I walked across the site and up the rickety stairs to the dorm rooms, the men were sitting on their beds, dressed and eagerly awaiting my arrival. However, one evening, no one gave the warning, so when I entered the door, one of the men was sitting on the bed in his underwear. His fellow bunkmates hit him and told him to get dressed because "we have a visitor." He looked up from his game, laughed, and said, "Who? *Zhihui* [my Chinese name]?" and kept playing. People laughed, and that was the end of it. This interaction made me realize that they had been "preparing" the dorm for me and that our relationship had reached a new stage in which my gender and nationality could take a backseat in my interactions with these construction workers.

Many times, I felt that because I am a woman, I was not taken seriously by many of the men. However, this was more of a benefit to my research than a detriment because most managers, labor contractors, and government officials did not see my presence as a threat (McDowell 1992). They were more likely to see me as an "innocent" student or "ignorant" woman rather than as a "knowledgeable" researcher, which led them to speak freely around me. This was especially true when I was sitting with a group of men who were discussing business. Generally, they did not speak to me, but only to each other. In front of me, they openly discussed illicit topics such as how to move payoff money, how much money to offer a worker who was permanently injured and how to cuts costs on materials. Until their business was complete, these men generally ignored me aside from offering a smile as I refilled their glasses and throwing an occasional glance at the Chinese characters I practiced writing as I listened. After concluding their conversation, the men then turned to me to ask about life in the United States, my background, and my opinions about China while expressing amazement at my Chinese language ability.

Most others also viewed me as an "innocent student" or "ignorant woman." As a result, my neighbors, coworkers and friends were quite protective of me. If someone came to the neighborhood looking for me, they would not give out my information or tell people where I lived. Instead, they would collect the person's name and number and give it to me. If I had a guest and it was getting late, they would tell my guest to head home and hint that I should get some rest. With some close friends in my neighborhood, I was able to move beyond these stereotypes. These friends helped me adjust to China by allowing me to fully participate in their lives—joining their families for dinner, watching movies and playing cards together, and loaning money back and forth. They would give me vegetables, mend my clothes, and fix my bike without charging me. In exchange, I would let them use amenities in my apartment, watch over their vegetable or bike stand while they ran to get lunch or to use the bathroom, and watch their kids.

Because of my nationality, I found that at first, many people avoided saying anything that might be construed as negative about China because they wanted to protect their country's image with foreigners. However, once we developed a closer relationship, I think that it was easier for people to talk to me about negative things because I am not Chinese. They did not have to figure out what was the "correct" answer; they knew I didn't have a connection to the party or government so they did not have to worry about negative repercussions. Generally speaking, as soon as people found out that I am a white American, they assumed I was wealthy. People often asked why I was wearing shoes with holes; surely I could afford as many shoes as my heart desired! People also assumed that I wanted to take a taxi instead of a bus, that I wanted bottled water rather than boiled water (*kaishui*), that I would purchase my food in a Western supermarket rather than a street market or a Chinese market and that my stomach couldn't handle street food or spicy food. Ultimately, spending time living, eating, working, and playing alongside local people created moments in which they saw me as Zhihui, a friend, co-worker, or neighbor. These moments were fleeting but highly treasured. However, most of the time, I couldn't hide my gender, nationality, race, or class. Instead, I worked hard to be aware of this positionality and reflective about how it impacted my relationships, my interactions, and ultimately my research.

Power is related to positionality, but it is a more difficult issue to address honestly. As with other scholars, one of my impulses is to hide the exploitative aspects of participant observation and ethnography through the altruistic goal of shedding light on the most vulnerable of workers and giving voice to Chinese migrants (Smith 1988). However, as England (1994, 242) suggests, an important question about power is, "Can we incorporate the voices of 'others' without colonizing them in a manner that reinforces patterns of domination?" Power relations are embedded in our practice of constructing knowledge, leaving little room to break patterns of domination. Reflexivity is central to recognizing, acknowledging and minimizing the exploitative relationships that are inherent in our research models. The practice of reflexivity is used to monitor and audit the research process, but there is no clear pathway or guide, much like wading through a swamp (Finley 2002).

In my own research process, I have come to realize that power is difficult to address honestly because even when we are our most reflexive, exploitative relationships do not simply disappear. Reflecting on my positionality forces me to recognize that I am a researcher who has the power to enter and leave the web of relationships and conditions of life in the field; my subjects do not share this privilege. I am also forced to recognize that my privileged status makes it possible for me to travel around the globe and to meet and talk with "others" in order to better understand my world.

I am not a Chinese peasant. I cannot ever truly understand what it is like to be a migrant worker in China's informal urban economy. This is not merely because I am white or American. Because of their own particular positions of power and privilege Chinese researchers are in no better position to understand the lives of migrant workers; as the relationship between migrant workers and Chinese academics are also problematic. However, I am fairly confident that despite these differentials of privilege and power in the field, I have used methodologies that are sensitive to these inequalities and that yield powerful insights into the lives of migrant workers.

In the end, this study represents intrusions into the lives of migrants and only provides us with one of many possible representations of those lives. I am interested in issues of work, the relationships that form in the context of work, and how those relationships fit into a larger framework of the organization of production and social reproduction. In my research, I focus on the data that seem most relevant to those questions. I attempt to give these migrants a voice, but it is important always to remember that this voice is the product of our conversations and not theirs alone. I am the person choosing what quotes to use, when to use them, and how to translate and frame them. In this sense, my interpretation and analysis cannot be presented as the true "voice" of these migrants; neither can it be presented as a dialogue. Rather, it reflects my efforts to merge the voices of construction workers and our conversations with my sociological imagination and training.

Finally, I want argue that reflexivity must continue during the analysis of the data and the final stages of knowledge production, including its consumption. The goal of this study is not to have the reader feel pity for Chinese migrant construction workers but to reveal their struggles and capture the positive and negative elements of their lives and work. When I was in China conducting this field research through interviews, time spent on job-sites and in the enclave, and work as a cement mixer, I was immersed in the daily lives of these workers. This immersion enabled me to suppress my privileged perspective—at least temporarily—and the feelings of sympathy and pity evoked by that perspective. This allowed me to see that construction workers' lives were filled not only with bitterness, difficulty and struggle but also with love, laughter, and companionship. And despite the harsh conditions

I experienced, my life among migrant construction workers was filled with love, laughter, and companionship as well. Now that I am no longer embedded in that environment, I am occasionally hit with an overwhelming sense of sadness about the situations I describe in my writing. However, I realize that it is not the story that has changed but my perspective. Thus, I urge the reader to be aware of their own positionality and think critically about what they bring to their reading of this book.

Acknowledgments

This book is the product of many relationships and years of work. Most important, it exists because of the migrant workers in China who demonstrated immense kindness, opened their homes and lives, taught me, and watched out for me. It is to them I am most indebted.

I began the research for this book while in the Department of Sociology at the University of Wisconsin–Madison. I have endless gratitude for my strong mentors: Gay Seidman provided intellectual guidance and personal support. Myra Marx Ferree gave me the lifetime gift of a gendered lens, which colors both my academic and nonacademic world. Erik Olin Wright insisted on analytic rigor. Edward Friedman shared his golden nuggets of knowledge about China and reminded me that as much as we think we know, we know very little. There are many others at the university who offered support and contributed to the fertile intellectual environment. I am eternally grateful for the opportunity to be a part of their legacy.

Equally influential were Shen Yuan and Sun Liping at Qinghua University in China, who taught me about developments in Chinese sociology, how to maneuver in Chinese academia, and how to conduct research in their country. I also owe a deep debt to scholars of labor in China who produced examples of excellence for me to emulate and who paved the way for my work. There are too many to list, but I have been deeply influenced by the work of Katie Quan, C. K. Lee, Pun Ngai, Anita Chan, Li Zhang, Mary Gallagher, and Elizabeth Perry.

The training I received under the guidance of Sarosh Kuruvilla, Lowell Turner, and Harry Katz at Cornell University's School of Industrial and Labor Relations was invaluable. I am indebted to them for their support and encouragement, despite the fact that many of the workers and organizations I study do not fit traditional definitions of workers or unions. I am especially in debt to Sarosh Kuruvilla, who pushed me to look beyond the theoretical confines of industrial relations to the fields of political science and sociology. I am eternally grateful to Nathan Lillie, my research partner, who was the yin to my yang.

I was able to travel the long road of writing a book because of the immense guidance and support offered by colleagues. At the University of Akron I found a sociology department that was committed to creating a space for the diversity of methodologies. Rebecca Erickson, Kathy Felty, Valarie Callanan, and Matthew Lee fought with the administration to resist a tenure model that pushed faculty toward writing articles rather than books. Their unwavering support was instrumental in creating the space for me to write this book, and it has kept me going even when things looked less than optimistic. Furthermore, Kathy Felty was my qualitative methods guru. I followed her example and had the honor of being involved with, and influenced by, her Active Research Methods Lab, which provides top-quality qualitative training to students and professors.

My work continued because colleagues at Wayne State University, Heidi Gottfried, Nicole Pagan-Truillo, and David Fasenfest, read drafts and offered support as I tried to balance the demands of two young children and an academic career. My work also benefitted tremendously from the feedback I received after presenting it at a number of institutions, including the University of Michigan, Sun Yat-Sen University, South China Normal University, Brown University, and the University of California, Berkeley. I am also deeply thankful to Fran Benson, who encouraged me to write the book I wanted to write. When she received the manuscript, it was still very much a book in the making. She did not send me away; instead she was willing to work with me to move it forward. Most of the reviewers she found restored my faith in the academic review process. Rina Agarwala and other, anonymous reviewers read it with a close eye and provided detailed comments, constructive critiques, and thoughtful suggestions.

I owe a special thanks to my husband, Marcin Szczepanski. He has read and commented on endless drafts, offered emotional support, and taken on a lot of work associated with social reproduction. This has helped us move toward our goal of creating a family in which both of us can have meaningful careers and be engaged parents. Finally, he accompanied me to China many times and used his amazing talent with the camera to produce breathtaking photographs that capture moments in the lives of the workers whose stories are told within these pages.

Although all of these people and institutions have played an important role in the writing of this book, all mistakes, shortcomings, or other problems that may be found in this book are my own.

Building China

Chapter 1

Building China and the Making of a New Working Class

Of Cement and Cigarettes

Dan squats near the gate and takes a slow drag from his South Sea cigarette. These cigarettes, called *Zhongnanhai* in Chinese, are named after an imperial garden next to the Communist Party headquarters. The name is rightfully earned, given that these are purported to have been Mao Zedong's favorite cigarettes. When Dan exhales, the billow of smoke lingers in the hot, still Beijing air. Dan is from Hebei—a province that surrounds Beijing and a place where everyone seems to smoke South Sea cigarettes. He crushes the hot ash between his calloused, cement-caked fingers, rises slowly from squatting position, and returns to work.

Dan spends most of his day bent over with his back facing the sun as he swings a shovel, mixing and moving cement. In 2010, China used 57 percent of the global production of cement for less than 20 percent of the world's population, and between 2008 and 2010, it used more cement than the United States used during the entire twentieth century (Smil 2013, 91). As Dan works, a fine dust fills his lungs and covers his body in a white-gray sheen. Sweat drips from his forehead into this textured material that is the key ingredient in building China.

Cement is used in both mortar and concrete: it is the glue that holds things together and the substance that gives most buildings their shape. Similarly, migrants like Dan are the glue and substance of China's modern cities. Like cement, they are ubiquitous yet easily overlooked. The estimated 260 million migrant workers in China are concentrated in the cities, representing 25 percent of the population of Shanghai, 30 percent of Beijing, and 40 percent of Guangzhou. Like mortar, these migrants hold the cities together, doing all the menial jobs that make things hum: they are porters, food preparers and servers, domestic workers, nannies, cleaners, retail and street vendors, sanitation workers, and workers in manufacturing and, of course, construction.

These workers are also like mortar in that they connect the large cities of China's East Coast to the rest of the country. One can almost map the origins of workers on a jobsite based on the cigarettes they smoke. In addition to Dan's favored brand, South Sea (Zhongnanhai), which indicates his home province, Hebei, a quick glance around the jobsite reveals workers smoking Pride (Jiaozi) from Sichuan, Double Happiness (Shuangxi) from Shanghai, Happy Cat (Haomao) from Shaanxi, Jade Creek (Yuxi) and Red Tower (Hongta Shan) from Yunnan, and Red Sand (Baisha) from Henan.

Just as migrant construction workers build China's cities, so too are their lives built around their work in the cities. Dan is only nineteen. He did not go to high school, and like hundreds of millions of other migrant workers, he came to the city to follow his dreams and find his future. He has two major life goals: to have a family and to become rich. He traveled to Beijing to acquire the "three keys" that are necessary to realize his dreams: a key to an office, a key to a house, and a key to a car. To reach his goals, Dan must first work his way into a good job (the key to an office); in construction, this means striking out on your own to become the boss or a contractor. Then, he will be able to afford a house and a car, or at least a motorcycle. Dan is from a poor family, and it is almost impossible to find a bride without something to offer; in China today, a groom is expected to bring the three keys to the table. How many shovelfuls of cement will it take for him to reach his goals?

This morning, Dan woke at 6:00 a.m. and was on the jobsite working by 7:00 a.m. Along with millions of other migrants, he does this day after day, year after year. He sometimes hums a tune as he swings the shovel. In the cool morning hours, it is not uncommon to hear humming or songs throughout the jobsite or to see smiles on workers' faces. By midmorning, breaks for cigarettes and water are a part of the rhythm, breaking the monotony of mixing, shoveling, and hauling. Inhaled smoke, coupled with small sips of warm water, provides relief from the alkaline dust. It also gives the body a moment to rest, the mind a moment to wander, and the spirit a moment to recover.

Like the concrete used in the buildings, these migrants give cities their form. In doing so, they become part of the cities they build. Dan has worked in Beijing for almost two years but has saved little money. I look over at Anlin, who is also smoking a South Sea cigarette. He is fifty years old, and his back is permanently hunched from years of lifting and bending as he works piles of cement. His hands are coarse, his face and back are darkened from long days in Beijing's unrelenting sun, his arms are scarred by accidents, and his body is gaunt from arduous work with minimal food. He doesn't return home anymore; his wife left, and his children grew up without him as he worked year after year in cities chasing his dreams. Cigarettes and cement, like the songs of the Sirens, lure many migrant workers away from home and down this path.[1] They offer the irresistible promise of a "Chinese Dream," but like the sailors trying to reach the Sirens, the workers are destroyed in the process of trying to realize that dream.[2]

Dan and Anlin are part of the growing number of informal precarious workers who are building a new, modern China. In the process, these workers are not only erecting concrete buildings and changing the cities but also reshaping China's working class.

Constructing China: Urbanization, Migration, and Informalization

Historically, the process of building cities has been a people-driven response to demographic shifts. As people move into cities, buildings and structures are built to accommodate them, which is how most cities grow.[3] However, the current historical period has witnessed a shift in the process of urbanization from people-driven to capital-driven. In cities characterized by capital-driven growth, capital investment has moved from manufacturing and production into building and real estate (Harvey 1985). Construction becomes a strategy of capital accumulation, changing from providing a means to an end to becoming an end in itself.

China is the paradigmatic example of this process. Urbanization is the cornerstone of China's modernization project and a driving force behind the nation's economic growth. In places like India and Africa, urban land expansion is driven by urban population growth. By contrast, in China it is driven more by growth in the per capita gross domestic product (GDP), which accounted for almost half of China's urban land expansion between 1970 and 2000 (Seto et al. 2011). Accordingly, China's construction industry experienced a spectacular annual average growth rate of 22 percent from 2001 to 2008 (Huang, Lan, and Bai 2013), representing about one-fourth (US$1.4 trillion) of China's GDP (National Bureau of Statistics of China 2010). Recently, its output value has surpassed that of the construction industry in the United States, making it the largest in the world. China is projected to account for about one-fifth of the global construction industry within the next decade (Ai-ju 2011).

This massive building spree is literally and figuratively remaking China. It is restructuring space as some of the world's longest bridges, tallest buildings, largest dams, and most expansive manufacturing facilities spring up across the landscape. An important part of this restructuring involves the movement of people, as hundreds of millions of migrants leave rural areas for growing cities. By the end of 2011, over 50 percent of China's 1 billion people lived in urban areas, many of them large cities. There are 160 cities with more than 1 million people; four of these have more than 10 million, and two megacities, Shanghai and Guangzhou, have more than 20 million.[4]

The process of building China is also (re)making its working class. The workers who build and serve the cities, along with those who produce goods for the world to consume, are mostly migrant workers.[5] They, or their parents, grew up in the countryside; they are farmers who left the fields and migrated to the cities to find work. In China, migration is regulated by the *hukou* system. This system involves an internal passport that, among other functions, restricts mobility and requires that migrants register in their new location, even if it is a temporary one. However, many migrants do not register. These unregistered migrants are similar to illegal migrants in other countries in that they have no access to social welfare or public goods, and as unregistered residents, they technically have no right to be in the city.[6] One estimate suggests that unregistered migrants make up roughly 12 percent of the urban population (X. Wu 2005); another study reveals that in many of the larger cities of the East Coast, more than half the migrants are unregistered (FL. Wang 2005, 78).

Most unregistered migrants end up working in precarious jobs in the informal economy.[7] Informal work includes jobs that pay wages but do not conform to labor laws and regulations, along with self-employment in businesses that are not registered with the state (Williams and Windeband 1998).[8] In China, the informal sector has evolved in tandem with economic marketization, urbanization, and integration into the global economy. Informal employment has grown from 15,000 workers in 1978, when economic reforms began, to more than 168 million in 2006, now representing over 60 percent of total urban employment (P. Huang 2009). Migrant workers perform most of the informal work.[9] It is concentrated in specific industries, including the construction and service industries, and specific occupations, including street vending, domestic work, child care, and recycling.

Examining the construction industry provides us with an understanding how the forces of urbanization, migration, and informalization are reshaping both China and its workforce. This industry involves one-third to one-half of all migrant workers and is the number-one industry hiring male migrants.[10] Informal employment in construction has grown from roughly 17 percent in 1999 to an estimated 70 percent in 2008 (Wells and Jason 2010; Lu and Fox 2001). In sum, the construction industry is an important sector representing informal precarious work in urban China.

Moving beyond the Façade: Uncovering and Understanding Informal Work in China

In an effort to understand the dynamics of informal work in China's construction industry, I immersed myself in the everyday life and work of male migrant construction workers for almost a year in 2004–5, followed by three shorter follow-up visits between 2008 and 2012. During this time, I gathered data from four types of research sites: enclaves including the one where I lived; construction jobsites including those where I worked; street labor markets; and governmental and nongovernmental organizations that serve migrant workers in Beijing and Guangzhou. The process of choosing sites and gaining access was complex and required a multipronged approach, which is detailed in appendix A. This ethnographic method allowed me to explore some of the processes that shape this large and growing informal precarious workforce. It produced a rich tapestry of data that provide a unique lens into their everyday lives, work, and existence in the cities.

Most of my effort focused on construction workers. I spent most of my time on construction sites in Beijing, Shanghai, and Guangzhou (see appendix B).[11] In total, I interviewed 130 people: 83 people in 2004–5; 24 interviews in 2009; and 23 interviews in 2012 (see appendix C).[12] These interview data are supplemented by field notes and journals that include observations and insights gained from participating in the lives of workers in the enclaves and on the jobsites.[13] During the data collection process in Beijing, I mapped out informal employment in the industry, developed the concept of "employment configuration," and identified three different employment configurations. I continued data collection until saturation was reached, meaning that new interviews and observations were not yielding significant new insights or data. I then decided to collect data in both Shanghai and Guangzhou in an effort to determine whether Beijing was a unique case or if it resembled other cities. I found that the three employment configurations existed in the construction industry in all three cities, but the prominence of each varied across these places. Since the main purpose of this book is to define and describe employment configurations in the industry, I draw mostly from the rich data accumulated from research in Beijing, and then, in the final chapter, I discuss similarities and differences across the cities and how they can inform future research.

This book makes three main contributions to our understanding of informal work in China. First, it documents diversity in employment relations and the labor market. This diversity exists in spite of the fact that all of these workers are similar: they are all men who are unregistered migrants working informally in the construction industry in major cities in China. This book helps us make sense of that diversity and the diversity of informal precarious work more generally. Second, it expands our understanding of China's emerging labor regime, which is central to labor control, intimately related to the urbanization process, and ultimately linked to China's overall economic success. Finally, it shows how these migrants struggle against the disciplining process, contest exploitation, and protest in unique ways. Just as with other workers toiling under capitalism, important structural forces shape their work and lives but are not deterministic. Thus, this large, emerging segment of workers should not be overlooked when analyzing the complexities of class and class politics in China.

Mapping out Diversity of Informal Work: Employment Configurations

The diversity of employment arrangements and working conditions that I found among these informal precarious workers is surprising because the scholarship tends to focus, explicitly and implicitly, on the difference between the categories of formal and informal work. As Williams and Lansky's (2013) review of the literature reveals, informal employment is either framed in opposition to formal employment, or it is defined in terms of what it is not. In the absence of a strong definition, formal work is seen as standard employment offering decent pay and good working conditions, and informal work is seen as nonstandard employment characterized by low wages, poor working conditions, and harsh labor control regimes (Castells and Portes 1989; Sassen 1994).[14] However, the boundaries between formal and informal employment have become blurrier as standard employment relations unravel across the globe and are replaced by increasingly precarious employment arrangements such as contingent, contract, temporary, and part-time work (Carré 2000; Kalleberg 2000).[15] Studies documenting precarious employment arrangements reveal the growing diversity of these arrangements and the increasing number of people in the flexible labor force that feed the global economy. Yet the scholarship remains focused on formal (precarious) work arrangements, leaving informal workers mostly hidden (Vosko, MacDonald, and Campbell 2009). This is despite the fact that informal workers represent anywhere from 20 to 90 percent of nonagricultural employment (Gottfried 2013) and constitute the largest sector of the worldwide labor market (Agarwala 2009).

Informal workers are being pulled "out of the shadows" and recognized as an increasingly important segment of the working class in both developed and developing countries (Fernández-Kelly and Shefner 2006).[16] We know that they are concentrated in key occupations and industries as street vendors (Cross 1998a), domestic workers (Hondagneu-Sotelo 2001), waste pickers (Medina 2008), day laborers (Valenzuela 2003), and home-based workers

(Kantor 2003).[17] Scholars have also identified important differences between informal self-employment, also referred to as "own account" work, and informal wage employment (Williams 2013). These nuanced studies and the insights they provide into informal work and labor politics do not go far enough to differentiate this huge segment of the workforce. In part, limitations are the result of an industrial labor relations framework that largely excludes informal workers and their employment situations from our analysis (M. Chen and Vanek 2013).

One of the most intractable issues in research on informal employment arises from the concept of the "employment relationship," a legal category that by definition excludes informal work. The International Labour Organization (ILO) states: "The employment relationship is the legal link between employers and employees. It exists when a person performs work or services under certain conditions in return for remuneration."[18] As a result, labor laws create categories of *formal* precarious work (e.g., temporary, contracted, or part-time), and *informal* work remains undifferentiated. This framing also implicitly distinguishes between formal work as regulated and informal work as unregulated. This book challenges that assumption by showing that informal work, despite being outside the law, is indeed regulated, albeit in different ways.

Another limiting aspect of this framework is related to labor market models (M. Chen and Vanek 2013). Most scholarship on labor markets places formal work in the center and treats the informal market as a residue of a previous primitive form of capitalism or a cheaper substitute to formal employment (Williams and Round 2008). Informal workers are theorized as forced into informal work by *exclusion* from the formal economy or as choosing to *exit* the formal economy and voluntarily enter informal work because it offers desirable alternatives for workers and businesses and owners who are strangled by regulations (Perry et al. 2007). This framing focuses attention on the related "good/bad" job dichotomy and obscures the diversity of arrangements within and across the formal/informal divide.

In an effort to bring informal work back into our framework, overcome existing definitional and conceptual limitations, and make sense of the empirical diversity of employment arrangements, I have developed a new concept: "employment configuration." *An employment configuration is defined as a specific pathway into employment linked with a specific mechanism that regulates the employment relationship.* The term "pathways into employment" directs our attention to how informal workers find their jobs rather than on how they enter the informal economy, allowing us to unpack diversity in the labor market on the informal side of the formal/informal binary. Furthermore, identifying and naming the mechanisms that regulate the employment relationship moves beyond the legalistic definition to recognize that extralegal mechanisms also shape employment relationships. Finally, the term "employment configuration" links how workers find their jobs and how their employment relationships are regulated.

My ethnographic work in China's construction industry reveals clusters of experiences, which are grouped together into three distinct employment configurations among informal migrant workers (see table 1.1). In some cases, workers find jobs through large labor contractors with whom they do not have a direct link through social networks. In these cases, the employment relationship is established, mediated, and regulated through a contract labor system based on a standardized, widespread, yet informal agreement. The resulting employment configuration is called *mediated employment.* Workers who use their social ties to find work operate under a configuration of *embedded employment*, where their employment relationships are embedded in and regulated through social networks. Finally, workers who find employment through street labor markets face despotic employment relations

Table 1.1. Summary of employment configurations

Employment configuration	Labor market (pathway into employment)	Employment relations (mechanism of regulation)
Mediated	• Workers use large labor contractors to find jobs • Rural labor market	*Mediated* and regulated by contractors and contracted labor system
Embedded	• Workers use social networks to find jobs • Rural and urban labor market	*Embedded* in social networks and regulated by these networks
Individualized	• Workers use street labor markets to find jobs • Urban labor market	*Individually* subordinated to unadulterated market forces and regulated mainly by violence or threat of violence

rooted in unequal power relations due to unchecked market forces. Employment relations in this case are mainly regulated through violence or the threat of violence, in what I label *individualized employment*.

I uncovered only three types of employment configurations among informal workers in the construction industry, but there may be more, especially if we include formal work. The number and types of configurations may also vary across construction industries in different countries or across different industries within a country. Exploring these possibilities will require additional research and comparative work.

The chapters to follow provide rich details that flesh out these definitions. They analyze the diversity of work situations experienced by these informal workers and show how most workers enter into and remain within one specific employment configuration. The focus on diversity within informal work rather than across the formal/informal divide (Nee, Sanders, and Sernau 1994) helps us understand why some workers are extremely mobile and others much less so. It also sheds light on how and why social networks operate differently among different groups of informal workers, in some cases operating as important tools for recruitment (Pun and Lu 2010), and in other cases, as a burden avoided by contractors (Menjivar 2000; Guang 2005). In sum, the concept of employment configuration is robust in that it offers additional analytical leverage and captures a broader range of employment relations, expanding our framework to include informal workers.

China's Labor Regime and the Spatial Politics of Production and Social Reproduction

China's integration into the global economy is characterized by a production system and a labor regime that successfully competes against, and in many ways out performs, flexible production and traditional Fordism. I argue that this success is, in part, based on the creation of a low-cost precarious workforce accomplished through spatially merging and separating (1) production, (2) daily reproduction, and (3) social reproduction of labor in ways that lower the daily costs of labor reproduction and eliminate the need for employers to pay a wage that can reproduce labor.[19]

As China's economy has grown, China's workers have received a shrinking piece of the expanding economic pie. Labor's share of the GDP has declined from 53 percent in 1990 to 39.7 percent in 2007 (Li 2007). This stands in stark contrast to most other countries, where labor's share of GDP usually ranges from 60 to 80 percent (Li 2007). This is possible because China's market economy has unique features that make it different from Western capitalism and different from capitalism in East Asia. One of the unique features of "capitalism with Chinese characteristics" is the "grabbing hand of the state," which works with capital to disenfranchise both peasants and workers (Y. Huang 2008, 283). One way that this happens is by spatially merging and separating production, daily reproduction and social reproduction of labor in ways that create precarious workers both on and off the jobsite and lower the overall costs of labor.

China's entrance into the global economy and the emergence of a new labor regime has included a protracted process of unmaking the "old" industrial working class while simultaneously making a new industrial working class (Lee 2007). The old industrial working class, shaped during the Maoist period, worked under a labor regime characterized by a socialist social compact anchored by the *danwei* system. In this labor regime, production and social reproduction of labor were merged as state-owned enterprises not only provided jobs but also meted out housing, health care, education, retirement, and access to cultural events. During the period of economic restructuring, which peaked between 1995 and 2001, employment in state-owned enterprises dropped from 113 million to 67 million (Giles, Park, and Cai 2006). Those who remain employed face precarity as their labor has become commodified through a smashing of the "iron rice bowl" and the separation of production from social reproduction of labor. Their employment is now girded by new labor law based on "the market-oriented, voluntaristic and individualistic 'labor contract'" (Friedman and Lee 2010, 509).

At the same time, a new industrial working class and an associated labor regime are emerging as the combination of global capitalism and altered legacies of socialism draws peasants from the fields into the factories and commodifies their labor under a dormitory labor system operating within this new legal labor regime.[20] The dormitory labor system produces a large permanently young, predominately female, temporary workforce that feeds the export-oriented manufacturing industry in South China (Pun 2007). Production and social reproduction are spatially configured quite differently from the old state-owned enterprise sector. In this sector, the state is also a central actor as production and social reproduction are *spatially* separated through institutions such as the *hukou* system, under which most peasants who move to the cities become temporary migrant workers. These temporary migrants work in the cities (production), but their access to social services, welfare, and public goods remains tied to their hometowns (social reproduction).

On another level, employers are central actors as they (re)structure employment to merge and/or to reconfigure production and daily reproduction under the dormitory labor regime in ways that benefit capital. This is done by cramming dozens of workers into single rooms, opting for low-quality food prepared in vast quantities, and eliminating the need for transportation. These arrangements also allow employers to extend their control over work and free time, which increases exploitation and working time and facilitates just-in-time flexible production practices (Pun and Smith 2007). The dormitory system, in conjunction with state policies, such as those mentioned above, shifts social reproductive costs back to rural areas. This is accomplished by hiring and housing only young single women, or individuals, rather than families.[21] In many cases, these arrangements require women to return to their hometown to marry and have children, and then, if they resume work, their children must be left behind to be cared for by relatives or grandparents (Murphy 2002). In creating these new industrial workers, one process spatially merges production and daily reproduction, and the second spatially separates production and social reproduction of labor. Taken together, they lower the daily costs of labor reproduction and eliminate the need for a wage that can reproduce labor.

The concept of *employment configuration* deepens our understanding of China's emerging labor regime by expanding beyond factory workers to include informal workers in the analysis. These informal workers are not toiling under a disintegrating socialist social compact or under the newly emerging legal regime accompanied by a dormitory labor system. Informal workers face a different set of constraints, and as the three employment configurations outlined in this book capture, there are multiple ways that production, daily reproduction, and generational or social reproduction are merged or reconfigured.

Mediated employment represents a gendered variant of the dormitory labor regime found in factories: one produces a cheap, predominately male, long-term but flexible workforce, and the other creates a young, predominately female, short-term flexible workforce. At the same time, both undermine families as they compel workers to migrate as "individuals" rather than as members of families. The costs of generational social reproduction is pushed onto extended family and hometown communities as production, which occurs in the urban areas, is spatially separated from social reproduction, which is carried out in the rural areas, or is eliminated.

The second employment configuration, embedded employment, offers an example of how production and social reproduction of labor can be merged in a qualitatively different way. In this employment configuration, production and daily reproduction are separated, but for the most part, both production and social reproduction occur in the cities. Migrants working in embedded employment are dating, getting married, setting up homes, getting pregnant, having children and, in some cases even raising children and retiring in the cities. This is not to deny their tenuous existence, or that some aspects of social reproduction are still forced back to the rural areas. However, this spatial re-uniting of production and social production in the cities creates dense social networks and helps these migrant workers develop social capital in the cities. As a result, social networks play an important role in creating an informal safety net and shape work relationships as mechanisms that emanate out of these social networks regulate employment and control the labor process. In the third employment configuration, individualized employment, social reproduction is effectively eliminated and daily reproduction is precarious as workers just struggle to survive.

The concept of employment configurations also captures how China's emerging labor regime not only lowers labor costs through rearranging the relationship between production and social reproduction but also lowers costs through increasing the precariousness that workers face both on and off the job. The spatial (re)arrangements of production and social reproduction under each employment configuration influence how migrants are integrated into cities and reshape relationships with their hometowns. As a result, life in the cities is experienced differently for migrants depending on their employment configuration: those in mediated employment live in a city of walls; those working in embedded employment live in a city of villages; and those in individualized employment live in a "city of violence." It also changes their migratory patterns and relations with hometowns. Workers who live on jobsites year after year in a "city of walls" become disconnected from their hometowns but do not become integrated into the cities; workers who live in a "city of villages" become tenuous settlers because of their lack of rights; and workers who live in a "city of violence" tend to be highly mobile, "floating" from city to city trying to evade trouble and find work. These different migratory patterns help explain why, in some cases, their connection to their hometown and the land continues to provide a kind of safety net, while in other cases, this link is more or less severed.

Finally, as we will see, the spatial merging and reconfigurations of production, daily reproduction, and social reproduction intensifies not only work and work control but also shapes conflict and protest among workers and between workers and employers.

Informal Workers, Class Politics, and Protest

The third and final major finding of this study is that these informal workers, while constrained by their employment configuration, are not rendered powerless, unorganizable, or impotent in terms of protest. In fact, protests actions range from everyday acts of resistance to participation in organized protests and formal organizations. They vary in targets and strategies; some utilize authorized channels and engage in tolerated protest behavior, and others push the boundaries. These protests and struggles, which are part of the developing dynamics of class politics in China, can only be understood in the context of the changing spatial organization of production and social reproduction under globalization within this specific national context.

Scholars have used the concept of labor regime to link the regulation of labor and the social reproduction of labor and show how it influences the form of labor protest and struggle (Lee 200; Buroway 1985).[22] As a result, we know a good deal about class politics and protests among China's industrial workers, but we know much less about class politics and protest among informal workers in China. The "old" industrial workers created out of Mao's Communist Revolution engage in "protests of desperation" as the social compact underpinning the arrangements in their work and lives disintegrates (Solinger 1999; Hurst 2004; Lee 2007). At the same time, "new" industrial workers are created as peasants leave the fields and enter the factories. In the process of becoming workers and citizens of the city, they engage in "protests against discrimination," which have gained legitimacy through the new regulatory labor regime (Lee 2007). The variation in the form of protests among these workers is attributed to the different labor regimes, and specifically to the "diverse modes of state regulation of labor and the system of social provision outside of waged work" (12).

However, industrial factory workers, both old and new, represent only a relatively small segment of the overall working population, and even at their peak in the mid- to late 1990s, they represented less than 15 percent of all workers in China (Evans and Staveteig 2009).[23] In contrast, other segments of the working class, such as those in the service sector and informal sector, are much larger and growing faster. This book expands our understanding of China's emerging labor regime by mapping out informal work and developing the concept of employment cofiguration, it then uses this conceptual map to help us understand struggles and protests by informal workers.

I use the concept of employment configuration instead of labor regime because it allows me to add a spatial analysis. The concept of employment configuration captures the diverse modes of regulation of informal work and how they are linked to different kinds of social provisions outside of waged work, but then nests this within a macro analysis of the production of urban space; and just as with formal work, it is then used to help us explain different kinds of protests. As such, protests among workers in mediated employment share similarities with migrant factory workers toiling under the dormitory labor regime; whereas protests among construction workers in embedded employment are more similarities with those of the laid-off factory workers in North China.

Protests among informal workers in mediated employment are somewhat similar to "protests of discrimination" by migrant factory workers described by Lee (2007), in that the main grievances are about wages and insurgent identities linked to exploitation and discrimination. At the same time, these workers in mediated employment are informal, without contracts or access to the law, so their protests do not include legal mobilization. They turn to collective protests which are different from factory workers in that they are not garnering structural power from their position in the economic system nor are they amassing associational power from an organizing into a union or labor organization. Instead, their protests take the form of "public dramas" which draw attention to their plight and gain support through claims-making that appeals to cultural values and moral norms, creating symbolic power.

In contrast, protests among informal workers in embedded employment are "protest of disruption" and in some ways look like "protests of desperation" by factory workers in state-owned enterprises under the disappearing socialist contract (Lee 2007). In both cases, workers take to the streets and cause public disruptions that interrupt normal function of society. In both cases, their grievances are not related to their own work but rather are centered on issues of citizenship, broadly defined. However, an important difference is that the protests that these informal workers participate in are outside of the routinized contentious bargaining that has become a hallmark of China's authoritarianism (Chen 2011). For informal workers in embedded employment, their work and lives are intimately connected to both the city and their hometowns. Social reproduction of labor takes place not only in the city, where these workers live their lives, but in some ways it is also forced back to their hometowns, where their citizenship and social rights remain.[24] It is in this context that the contradictions of living in the city while lacking citizenship and the right to be a part of the city creates a tenuous existence which becomes salient and leads them to participate in "protests of disruption." Finally, in individualized employment, worker ties to family and community are severed, and both production and social reproduction are precarious. In these conditions, and in the face of a despotic labor regime, these workers still carry out everyday forms of resistance but rarely participate in collective action as workers or as citizens.[25]

This book also adds to our understanding of informal workers' resistance and class politics and protest by providing a case study of resistance among informal workers toiling under an authoritarian state where basic labor rights are not recognized. The few studies on organizing and protests among informal workers in China are pessimistic. Lee and Shen (2011) suggest that in China's political context, collaboration between informal migrant workers and nongovernmental organizations (NGOs) results in antisolidaristic tendencies rather than collective power and action. Pun and Lu (2010) examine collective action among construction workers and argue that the construction industry does not present a "normal" employment relationship because there is "no boss, no employer directly responsible for employment practices." As a result, "the exceptional practices involved in the rapidly changing construction industry induce angry, largely impotent collective actions by construction workers" (158). However, as Cho (2013) suggests in her study of laid-off workers, it may be helpful to move beyond defining worker resistance in term of class struggle based on the relation of production, and if we can do so, "what we witness in China is not the absence or incompleteness of resistance but a different style of resistance" (6).[26] This is important given that informal workers in China, like in many other areas of the world, tend not to join unions or use the strike and traditional protest forms that are popular with the formal industrial working class.

There are multiple reasons why these workers, especially informal workers, do not join unions or participate in typical forms of labor protest. First, they are generally seen as weak and unorganizable, and their protests are deemed impotent. They are considered difficult to organize because they are not protected by labor laws. They are also poor, underprivileged, without clear or defined employers, and change jobs frequently (Jhabvala 2013). All these factors lead to workers who are "widely dispersed, disconnected, and unregulated," creating a fragmented and heterogeneous workforce that poses challenges to collective solidarity and organizing (K. M. Roberts 2002, 22). Furthermore, many informal workers feel that unions and other formal labor organizations are not a good fit because informal workers often lack the legal standing necessary to pursue legal action used by unions, and their needs differ from those of traditional workers (Jhabvala 2013; Wells and Jason 2010). Also, unions are often not serious about organizing informal workers, ignoring them or denying them a voice (Chinguno 2010; Liu 2010). As a result, informal workers do not turn to traditional mobilization strategies and institutions. In fact, Agarwala suggests that these traditional forms of organizing and protest are not widespread among informal *or* formal workers.

> For decades, industrialized workers fought to enter into an institutional structure that provided some play for collective interests; this institutional structure formalized workers' identities and status through legislation designed to protect them against employer exploitation. Their efforts, while laudable, have affected only a minority of the world's workers. Now, due to the industrial restructuring of the 1980s and 1990s, even the small global share of formally protected workers is diminishing. These changes have brought scholarship of labor movements to a critical juncture by questioning traditional mobilization strategies and institutions that rely on formal state protections and employer accountability. (2008, 377)

In contrast to formal workers, informal workers create a wide range of organizations beyond traditional unions, including worker cooperatives such as those created by waste pickers in Brazil (Medina 2008); worker associations such as the Self-Employed Workers Association (SEWA) organized by women in India (Kapoor 2007); worker centers like those established by day laborers in the United States (Fine 2006); and nontraditional unions such as the associated unions organized by street vendors in Mozambique (Schurman et al. 2013).

Informal workers are also more likely to target the state than employers (Chun 2009; Agarwala 2008), and although they struggle with class-based issues, they often make claims using the rhetoric of citizenship or human rights (Agarwala 2008; Milkman 2011). Finally, sometimes informal workers engage in individual or quiet collective acts of resistance (Tripp 1997; Cross 1998b; Whitson 2007), and at other times they turn to more dramatic forms of collective action (Kudva 2009; Bayat 1997; Milkman and Wong 2000). I argue that their struggles, protests, and organizing, far from being impotent or ineffective, play an important role in emerging class politics in China.

In sum, there are at least three important segments of China's emerging working class, each with unique characteristics. The factory workers in the Rustbelt are part of the working class but are not proletarians in the Marxian sense, in that they were simultaneously workers and owners of the means of production under the socialist system (Walder 1984). The migrants in the Sunbelt who work in factories owned by global capital do not yet constitute a class; instead, they are a class in the making (K. Chan and Ngai 2009). Finally, these informal workers are part of the precariat and should also be included in our analysis of China's emerging working class.

China's emerging labor regime represents a fragmented working class but that does not make it passive or impotent. While factory workers participate in protests of desperation and protests of discrimination, informal workers participate in protests using public dramas and protests of disruption. Although their protest and struggle differ from those of traditional workers, these informal workers challenge the power of global capital, confront state repression, and restore dignity to peasants finding their place in the urban economy. These struggles make their journeys out of the fields and into cities less fatalistic and earn them an important place in history.

Outline of the Book

Chapter 2 presents important background information about China's *hukou* system, migration patterns, and construction industry. A brief overview of the system, how it has changed, and what it looks like today is followed by a categorization of the types of migrants based on citizenship rights and a summary of the changes in migration laws and patterns over time. The chapter closes with a more detailed look at the construction industry and how its reorganization during the reform period allowed it to absorb a significant portion of the new migrant workforce.

Chapters 3, 4, and 5 use empirical data to describe the three employment configurations that characterize informal work in the construction industry. Each chapter introduces the employment configuration, defines the labor market (pathway into employment) and identifies the main mechanisms of regulation. The chapters then describe the links between patterns of entrance into employment and how employers regulate their labor. These chapters also show how employment configurations shape migrant workers' spatial integration into the cities and their migratory patterns. Chapter 3 details *mediated employment*, the contracted-labor system on which it is based, and the intricate relationship between this employment configuration and the rural-urban divide. Chapter 4 outlines *embedded employment* with a focus on the different kinds of social networks that shape this pathway into employment and related mechanisms regulating this employment such as kinship obligation and bounded solidarity. Chapter 5 presents *individualized employment*, showing that it is the most exploitative form of employment, in many ways similar to unfree labor. This employment configuration is characterized by high rates of nonpayment of wages and the use of violence or threat of violence to regulate employment.

Chapter 6 looks at how these informal workers organize and protest despite the fact that they are often considered unorganizable. It shows how historical contingency alongside specific employment configurations shape protests, explaining why organizing and protest activities take the form of daily collective resistance punctuated by explosive collective action. It does this by presenting and analyzing some of the more salient issues for informal workers in construction, such as nonpayment of wages (wage theft) and right to livelihood; the former is usually considered a workers' issue, and the latter is often defined as a citizenship issue. However, these lines are blurred among informal workers for whom work and living spaces are merged. The production of space and the organization of both production and social reproduction structure the politics of informal employment.

The closing chapter compares the contours and content of precarious work and precarious existence across the three employment configurations. It considers how these configurations compare to notable employment arrangements in different places and industries across the globe. The chapter concludes by exploring how protests among informal workers are similar to and different from protests among other kinds of workers. These informal workers—who represent a large segment of the emerging workforce—do not fit the traditional model of an industrial wage worker and are not being incorporated into a new legal framework under China's decentralized legal-authoritarian regime. This may lead some to consider this segment of China's new proletariat as the "precariat," an emergent social force based on vulnerability, insecurity, and uncertainty (Standing 2011). However, this precarious informal workforce is not a "new class" in that it was also a prevalent segment of the working class in China before the Communist revolution. It has reemerged as a central component of China's economic success, and in turn, an important source of labor resistance.

Chapter 2

The *Hukou* System, Migration, and the Construction Industry

The monumental rise of migrant labor in China is shaped by China's *hukou* system, which operates as an internal passport system that links citizenship rights and welfare benefits to birthplace (Solinger 1999; Chan and Zhang 1999). During Mao's time, the system assigned three identifiers to every citizen at birth: (1) *hukou* status as agricultural or nonagricultural; (2) a home place designated as rural or urban; and (3) an identification number. *Hukou* status and home place both are inherited from one's parents. For example, if a child is born in Beijing, but her parents' *hukou* registration is in Shandong, the child's *hukou* registration will also be in Shandong. Similarly, if the parent's *hukou* status is agricultural, the child's status will be agricultural.[1] Citizenship rights, including access to social welfare benefits, were based on status and linked to place of registration; however, over time, access to rights under China's *hukou* system has become varied and complex.

The *hukou* system is a central institution shaping Chinese society. It is "among the oldest, longest-lasting political institutions dating back 25 centuries" (FL. Wang 2005). Contradictions and complexities are an artifact of its long history. During different historical periods, the *hukou* system has been used for economic planning and resource allocation, central planning, taxation, control, mobility restriction, discipline, population control, and land policy. The system has followed maternal lines at some times and paternal lines at others. In some periods, the *hukou* system was disassociated from birthplace and instead linked with current residence.

The *hukou* system took on the form of modern legislation during the Kuomintang (KMT) government of the early twentieth century (FL. Wang 2005) and was solidified during the Maoist era under the Communist Party (CCP). The CCP had three main goals in implementing and modifying the *hukou* system. First, to root out state enemies, the *hukou* system included a special *hukou* class for those suspected of disloyalty, allowing authorities to keep track of these people. Second, the *hukou* system played a major role in the implementation of collectivization through food rationing and the subsidy system put into place in the mid-1950s. The CCP linked *hukou* registration to the distribution of public goods and social services including housing, child care, schooling, and medical care (Feng 1997). These were also linked to the state labor bureau's system for assigning employment positions (Guang 2001). Third, the *hukou* system limited and controlled the movement of people. Despite significant disparities in the level and quality of social services and employment opportunities between rural and urban areas, individuals had few opportunities for physical relocation apart from state-directed movement (Cheng and Selden 1994).

All of these aspects of the *hukou* system contributed to the emergence of a central feature of life in China during the Maoist era: China's bifurcated class society across the rural/urban divide. As one scholar notes: "Household registration, at the core of a whole set of institutional mechanisms controlling food, housing, work and travel, enabled a differential treatment of people according to whether their place of birth and residence was rural or urban. From then on peasants were treated as second-class citizens, despite the Maoist rhetoric on peasant values" (Florence 2004, 43).

The main mechanism through which this differential treatment occurs is government control over and redistribution of resources. The CCP consistently allocates more and better resources to urban areas (Cheng and Selden 1994). As a result, urban residents have access to higher-quality schools, health care, jobs, and food. They also have access to better infrastructure such as public transportation, roads, sports and entertainment facilities, airports, water and sewage systems, and electricity. In Maoist China, the *hukou* policy firmly tied people and citizenship rights to place, so people were born into their "class" (Naughton 2007). However, the economic reforms that began in 1978 changed the *hukou* system and ushered in a new era.

One of the earliest and most important changes of the reform period was the adoption of the Household Contract Responsibility (HCR) system, which rearranged agricultural production and allowed peasants to produce for profit.[2] Peasants had been producing under the commune system, which tied their labor to the land, and production was governed by a quota system. This changed under the HCR system such that peasants still had a small quota to fill, but most of their production was now for the market. This new system untied labor from land, giving peasants the freedom to profit from their own labor (X. Wu 2005). These changes created surplus labor in the rural areas, where 85 percent of the population resided, opening the possibility for new migration flows sanctioned by the government through a combination of three laws implemented in 1985. First, new regulations permitted farmers to move to local towns to start businesses and issued them "self-supplied food grain" *hukous*. Second, the government issued all citizens identity cards (IDC) and allowed them to be used as proof of identification (in lieu of the *hukou* passbook issued to each household) (Yusuf and Saich 2008). Finally, the CCP created a new *hukou* status by allowing cities to issue Certificates of Temporary Residence (*zanzhuzheng*) to peasants who entered the city for work.[3] Temporary residence status is granted for one year, after which it must be renewed (Chan and Zhang 1999). Taken together, these reforms along with other changes created the foundation for massive migration within the confines of a reformed *hukou* system. Migration flourished, growing from less than 30 million migrant workers in 1980 to about 80 million in 1990 (Liang and Ma 2004) to more than 120 million in 2004, reaching approximately 262 million workers by 2012 (National Bureau of Statistics of China 2012a).

The purpose of the *hukou* system shifted during the reform period.[4] It is still used to monitor and manage the movement of people (Chan and Zhang 1999) and as a tool of discipline and control (He 2003; FL. Wang 2004). However, it is also used by the state to regulate the economy in new ways (F. Cai, Du, and Wang 2003). Furthermore, as the system has evolved it now maintains and perpetuates the rural/urban economic disparities created under the Maoist-era planned economy by creating a segmented urban labor market made up of privileged urban citizens and disadvantaged temporary migrant labor (Solinger 1999). As Chan (2009, 204) points out: "What is unique about migration in China is that the two aspects of internal migration (movement and citizenship) can be totally disparate; i.e., one can move to a new place (for example, because of a job change) but can be permanently barred access to community-membership-based services and welfare."

Hukou reforms have allowed peasants to migrate into cities while denying them access to social welfare such as education, health care, and housing subsidies. Temporary residents are not granted urban citizenship, nor are their children, making it impossible to put down "roots" in the cities. The end result is a large pool of cheap, temporary, flexible labor that is an important engine of China's economic growth.

Today, the *hukou* system stands as a strong legitimate institution, though it continues to undergo reforms that increase its complexity. Specifically, the *hukou* is becoming localized, which means that local governments are gaining the power to decide what kind of *hukou* to grant migrants, which criteria to use to regulate migration, and how many migrants to allow into their jurisdiction (Chan and Buckingham 2008). Shifts in national and local regulations have created internal contradictions in the policies and practices that define the relationship between migrants and the state. These contradictions are part of what makes *hukou* an enduring institution by creating uncertainty in current practices while opening opportunity for ongoing change.

Migrants and Citizenship Rights

Hukou reform created a large new segment of the working class known as "peasant workers" or "migrant workers."[5] In 2009, the government estimated the total number of migrants to be approximately 230 million, or between 15 and 17 percent of China's population. More than half (145 million) are interprovincial migrants, meaning they left their home province (NBSC 2009).[6] These migrants are concentrated in larger cities, especially those on the East Coast. In Beijing, migrants are estimated to represent about a fourth of the city's population, and cities in Guangdong province, such as Shenzhen, often have migrant populations that outnumber locals (Y. Wang 2005). However, not all migrants are the same.

A person becomes a migrant when he/she leaves the place where he/she is registered under the *hukou* system. As a result, scholars often discuss two broad categories of migrant workers: *hukou* and non-*hukou* migrants (K. Chan, Liu, and Yang 1999). Migrants who formally transfer their local residency are *hukou* migrants; those who do not receive formal residency in the host community are called non-*hukou* migrants.[7] For this study, *hukou* migrants are called permanent migrants, and non-*hukou* migrants are divided into two categories based on citizenship rights: special migrants and temporary migrants. In addition, the category of temporary migrants includes registered and unregistered migrants (see table 2.1 for a summary).

It is difficult to estimate number of migrants in each category or even the total number of migrants in China. The estimates are problematic for several reasons. First, the definition of migrant varies from study to study. Second, surveys often do not include migrants who have been in their host location for less than six months. Third, sampling procedures that miss unregistered migrants may also result in the underestimation of the overall migrant population and of specific subgroups. Fourth, migration policy is dynamic, so new statuses for migrants are constantly emerging.

The first type of migrant, permanent migrants, move into the city and change both their place of registration and, if still in existence, their *hukou* status (from agricultural to nonagricultural).[8] This group is regulated by policies dictating requirements for changing one's status and is subject to quotas. The most common pathways to a status change are through state-owned enterprise recruitment, attending a college or university, or promotions within

Table 2.1. Migrants by types and population estimates

Types of migrant	Estimated population of migrant group
Permanent migrants	4–10 percent of total migrant population (estimated for 1990s). Roughly 20 million in 2007 without much change across time. (K. Chan 2011)
Special (*hukou*) migrants	No good estimates because issued at local level. Probably no more than 10 percent of migrant population and most likely much less but growing.
Temporary registered	114–28 million in 2006. (K. Chan 2011)
Temporary unregistered	12% of total urban population and up to 50% of population in larger cities (estimates based on 2004 [and later] statistics). (FL. Wang 2005; Cooke 2008; P. Huang 2009)
Total migrant workers	262 million (2012), 230 million (NBSC 2009)

the Party (K. Chan and Zhang 1999). Once the *hukou* change is complete, migrants become the equivalent of urban citizens with full entitlement to all state benefits in the city. The number of permanent migrants is quite low. Wu and Treiman (2004) used a discrete-time hazard-rate model to calculate the likelihood of *hukou* conversion and found that when the CCP first came into power, the conversion rate was relatively high at 4 percent. By the early 1960s, under a very restrictive policy, conversion rates fell to less than 1 percent and remained there through the mid-1990s, the last period covered in Wu and Treiman's study.

The second type of migrant, "special" migrants, are migrants who have obtained one of the new *hukou* statuses that entitle them to some state-provided benefits and often provide some future possibility of full conversion to urban citizen. In most cases, these are locally administered special status *hukous* that are awarded to rich migrants who can "buy" the *hukous* or to migrants with special technical or managerial skills. In 1994, Shanghai became one of the first cities to institute a special *hukou*, known as the *blue chop-hukou*. Individuals could apply if they made an investment of at least US$200,000 in Shanghai, if they bought an apartment meeting certain specifications, or if they had special professional or technical skills and had a three-year record of gainful employment (Wong and Huen 1998). Localities have increasingly relied on special *hukou* statuses to attract migrants with high human capital and to facilitate economic growth. This is done using point systems similar to those used for international migration (L. Zhang 2012). There are no good estimates of special-status *hukou* holders, but, although this group is growing, it probably comprises no more than 10 percent of the total migrant population.

The third type of migrant, "temporary migrants," consists of two subtypes: registered and unregistered. Peasants who cannot obtain a permanent *hukou* transfer or a special *hukou* status can often enter the city as temporary migrants. Registered temporary migrants are granted a one-year renewable "temporary residency." To migrate legally, temporary migrants must successfully navigate a number of permit and certificate requirements, especially in larger cities. Permit and certificate requirements by location, but they generally include: (1) ID card; (2) resident permit; (3) temporary work permit; (4) health certificate; and (5) family planning certificate or marriage certificate/status certificate. This documentation requires that peasants secure a job and housing arrangements in the city in advance. The costs of completing the documents range from three hundred to eight hundred yuan (about US$40 to US$100), a relatively large sum for Chinese peasants. The registration process is often employer-driven. If an employer wants to formally hire a migrant worker, that employer will make sure that the documents are filed and processed. Migrants who do not have an employer or whose employer does not wish to hire them formally typically do not register.

Despite being registered, these temporary migrants are *not* granted citizenship. They are legally allowed in the city to work, but their citizenship rights remain tied to their hometown. If they want to access social welfare such as health care, education, housing subsidies, or unemployment insurance, they must do so through their hometown governments. In the cities, they can access some public goods and social welfare such as public transportation, health care, and education by paying fees, but the fees are usually much higher than what locals pay and often are prohibitive.

Most migrants are either registered temporary migrants or unregistered temporary migrants. Cai, Park, and Zhao (2004) review the 2000 census data, which estimated the total number of migrants to be 131 million. The authors point out that about 40 percent of temporary migrants were rural-to-urban migrants, and 37 percent were urban-to-urban migrants. Urban-to-urban migration means that some migrants move from a large city like Shanghai to another large city like Beijing. These migrants likely already have a nonagricultural *hukou*. However, migrants from smaller cities may or may not have nonagricultural status, and they may or may not be able to transfer their *hukou* to the new urban location. If not, they are in a situation similar to that of rural-to-urban migrants in terms of citizenship. According to their definition, about two-thirds of rural-to-urban migrants are temporary migrants who did not change their official residence location. However, their study does not distinguish between registered and unregistered migrants.

Unregistered temporary migrants enter the city without legal documentation; it is most difficult to estimate the number of unregistered migrants because they are "missing" from official statistics. A general estimate suggests that unregistered migrants make up roughly 12 percent of the urban population (X. Wu 2005). However, if we look at specific cities, like those on the East Coast, unregistered migrants can represent up to 50 percent of the total population (FL. Wang 2005).[9] In part, the number of unregistered migrants in large cities is high because those cities have very stringent registration requirements for migrants. These local *hukou* policies do not have the intended effect of discouraging migration but instead create a large population of "undocumented" migrants (Swider 2014).

There are two main differences between unregistered and registered temporary migrants. First, unregistered migrants do not have a legal right to be in the city. If caught by police or urban security officers without documentation, unregistered migrants can be harassed, fined, jailed, and even deported from the city. Second, unregistered migrants work informally because they cannot be hired on a formal contract without proper documentation. One study of informal work in China reports that "at least 150 million workers are engaged in informal employment in the urban area, representing over 20 per cent of the total employment" (Cooke 2008, 5). Other studies estimate that informal employment represents 60 percent of urban employment and that most informal workers are either migrants or laid-off factory workers (Park and Cai 2011). Workers who are hired informally face precarious working conditions, a lack of written contracts, and a lack of access to insurance, retirement, and other social welfare benefits.

In summary, China's *hukou* system has evolved from a system with very little movement of people to a system with significant migration flows. In part, this is the result of reforms such as the reorganization of agricultural production, the elimination of food ration coupons, the uncoupling of employment and housing, the legalization of housing rentals, and the opening of the labor market beyond state-owned enterprises. However, key elements of the *hukou* system remain, and the current system still separates two key aspects of migration: the movement of people and the conferral of citizenship rights at the destination (K. Chan 2010). As a result, migrants live in cities where they have limited or no access to social services, jobs, or rights. Thus, the *hukou* reforms have created a paradox: new structures and institutions support migration without creating political channels for migrants to achieve legal citizenship. This contradiction has generated a large number of temporary and/or undocumented migrants in China's cities.

While much research has focused on the rural/urban divide and the difference between natives and migrants, this study focuses on the differences among migrants and pays specific attention to unregistered migrants. Due to the *hukou* system, unregistered migrants are illegal in their own country, deprived of rights in the city and often forced into informal employment. The next section explores how the rise of temporary migrant workers is intertwined with the growth of the construction industry.

China's Construction Industry and the Migrant Population

As in many of the world's global centers, the construction industry in China is dependent on a migrant workforce. In China, one-third to one-half of the total migrant population is believed to work in the construction industry (Solinger 1999). Construction is the number-one industry employing male migrant workers, who make up over 80 percent of the industry's total workforce. Furthermore, as in most countries, illegal/undocumented migrants are concentrated in the construction industry. Despite their importance to the industry, very few studies have examined migrants working in construction.[10] This section examines major changes in the construction industry from the Maoist regime to the reform period and then describes current employment conditions. One goal of this analysis is to depict both continuity and ruptures: continuity in that many legacies from the past continue to leave an imprint on the present form of the industry, and ruptures in that the rise of migrant labor is connected to the rapid growth of the construction industry.

Maoist Era Reforms: Nationalization and Vertical Integration

Shortly after the Communist Party came to power in 1951, the construction industry underwent thorough nationalization as part of the "Three-Anti, Five-Anti" campaigns.[11] This process subordinated construction enterprises to national government ministries. Nationalization of the construction industry dramatically increased employment in the industry but also magnified inefficiencies due to rigid vertical integration, organization of enterprises along specialty, and a mobile rather than geographically based labor force.

During this period, the central government issued five-year plans allocating labor, material, and technology to each industry under the control of a national ministry that allocated resources to projects in different geographical areas. This created a vertically integrated construction industry that operated without the profit incentive found in most capitalist market economies.

Vertical integration made it difficult to coordinate construction work occurring in the same location. One city could have independent construction projects led by different ministries and/or different levels of government. This sometimes led to an unintentional clustering of projects due to a lack of zoning or planning and a lack of coordination in terms of resources, transportation, or equipment. Construction enterprises were classified as either general contractors or specialized enterprises (similar to today); a general contractor subcontracted certain segments of the project to the special enterprises. Because the special enterprises were under the jurisdiction of a different government ministry, the general contractor had little or no authority over these subcontractors, making it difficult to have any effective control over the entire project (Yun 1956).

Furthermore, the Communist goal of full permanent employment contradicted the nature of the construction industry, which is seasonal and has geographically dispersed worksites. These contradictions created glaring inefficiencies (Chao 1968). For example, a construction enterprise under the Construction Engineering Ministry would be directed to do a project in a province in the northeast. The enterprise would move all necessary equipment, staff, workers and their families hundreds of miles to do the project. Once completed, they might be assigned to a project in the southeast. This required that all equipment, staff, employees, and their families be moved to the new location. In contrast, in market-oriented economies, construction companies are geographically based and draw from the local workforce rather than moving people from place to place.

These arrangements created a workforce that looked very different from the modern Chinese workforce. Its characteristics made it an obvious choice for later reforms. The Chinese workforce in 1956 was employed in large enterprises where the average number of employees per enterprise was 2,500 as compared to 2 to 40 people per enterprise in Western countries (Chao 1968). Also, the Chinese construction industry had a higher percentage of permanent workers and managers. These workers were assigned full-time jobs through government labor bureaus and made up a relatively large percentage of overall employment (F. Cai, Park, and Zhao 2004). However, in comparison to other industries within China, the construction industry had a high proportion of temporary employees. In 1953, temporary employment represented about 44 percent of the industry's total employment (Chao 1968). Furthermore, although the construction industry worked to create full-time, permanent, lifetime employment, sometimes referred to as "iron rice bowl" arrangements, it also displayed diversity in employment relations by hiring three different types of workers: permanent employees, temporary employees, and draft labor.

Permanent employees received compensation even when there were work stoppages beyond their control, such as material shortages, bad weather, or delays in the design or implementation of the project. They were assigned to a *danwei* and received benefits such as housing, education, and health care.[12] Temporary workers were recruited from the local workforce to supplement permanent workers on an as-needed basis. These temporary workers were generally of rural origin with low levels of education and training. Their compensation was calculated under the "pay as you work," or piece-rate, system. Finally, a significant segment of the industry workforce consisted of draft laborers. Draft laborers included peasants (who were mobilized in the winter when agricultural work was at a lull), military labor, and workers from labor reform camps or prisons. Draft labor was used most extensively on larger public work programs such as water projects and large transportation projects. Draft labor was not included in official labor statistics but was estimated to represent 3.5 million man-days of work in construction in 1958. These draft workers were poorly compensated, if at all, providing evidence that the construction industry has always relied on "unfree labor" to some degree. One scholar describes the system:

> Each worker was supposed to be compensated at a uniform rate—eight catties of grain each working day. As the scale of basic construction gradually increased, this measure lost its significance as an instrument of relief. It became instead an indispensable way of mobilizing labor resources in China or a method of using limited investment funds to cope with an ambitious industrialization program. The compensation rate lowered on several occasions to a level at which each mobilized worker would obtain only enough food to keep him alive. (Chao 1968, 138)

This structure of construction employment was unique in China in that few industries (other than mining) used draft labor or temporary labor, both of which are antithetical to the full-employment goals of the CCP. This employment structure made construction a target for reorganization during the reform era, with the goal of absorbing the new migrant labor force.

The Reform Era and Current Configurations

Most reforms in the construction industry took place in the mid-1980s and coincided with a substantial increase of migrant streams into cities. Early construction industry reforms built on the existing employment structure with the goal of hiring of migrant labor, quickly changing the composition of the workforce. Later reforms focused on quality control but had the effect of pushing increasing numbers of labor contractors and their workers into the informal sector.

The most dramatic changes in the construction industry's employment structure were the result of reforms in the mid-1980s.[13] The industry already had a relatively high number of nonstandard rural workers, so it was targeted by the government to absorb a significant portion of the new migrant workers who were flowing into cities. Accordingly, the government issued two important executive orders. First, in 1984, it issued an executive order called "The Separation of Management from Field Operations" (Qian and Hui 2004). This order reorganized the construction industry into three basic types of enterprises: general contracting companies, specialist companies, and labor-only companies. The accompanying order was called "Tentative Provisions for Construction Industry and Capital Investment Administration System Reform [1984] No 123." Among other things, these provisions required that state-owned enterprises reduce the size of their "fixed" or permanent workforce and disallowed hiring workers other than the skilled professionals necessary to keep the companies operating. All new construction jobs in state-owned enterprises were to be filled by contract workers.[14]

In practice, these two directives led to a bifurcated workforce. On the one hand, urban residents were hired by general contracting companies to fill administrative and technical positions, but hiring was done at a much slower pace. On the other hand, labor-only companies were formed, essentially as contractors who hired rural migrants to fill all fieldwork (construction jobsite labor) positions. Employment in these "labor-only" companies exploded. It did not take long for the reforms to significantly change the composition of the construction industry workforce. In 1980, there were about 10 million workers in the construction industry, including about 7.1 million urban workers and 3 million migrant workers. By 2001, about fifteen years after the reforms were initiated, urban workers in the construction industry numbered

7.33 million, and rural migrant workers numbered almost 30 million (Qian and Hui 2004).

In 1987, in an effort to control the growing construction labor force, the government set up an office in Beijing called the "Incoming Construction Force Administration Office." By 2001, the office had fifty workers and branches in districts and counties under the Beijing Municipality (Lu and Fox 2001). The office charged incoming workers service and document fees but offered additional services: legal, technical, and management training; and dispute settlement. The office requires contractors and subcontractors to hire "organized" labor rather than individualized labor, seeking to channel the labor force through various sending and receiving government agencies. Some scholars and practitioners suggest that this type of administration led to massive subcontracting in the industry.[15]

In the late 1990s, a series of reforms pushed many contractors and migrant workers into the informal sector. In 1997, the Construction Law was enacted, unifying the construction industry under a single set of regulations. It covered topics such as the procurement process, bidding, qualifying requirements of construction enterprises, safety, quality, and legal liability.[16] A new classification system regulated construction companies as specialists, general contractors, and labor contractors. There were twelve different types of general contractors, sixty types of specialists, and twelve categories of labor subcontractors. The goal of the new structure was to weed out inefficient contractors to avoid a situation in which too many firms made labor contracting "unreasonably competitive." Many observers suggest that as a result, a large part of the construction industry went underground or moved from the state sector to the informal sector rather than to the private but regulated sector (see figure 2.1).

Today, most workers do not use government agencies to find work in the industry. Instead, they use a variety of intermediaries ranging from large labor contractors, small contractors, social networks, and labor market bosses.

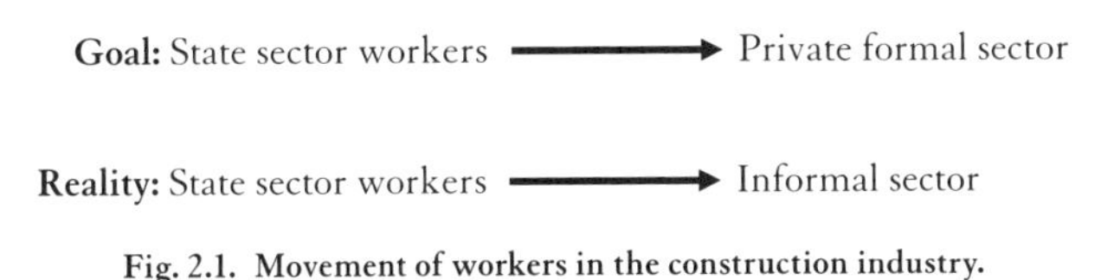

Fig. 2.1. Movement of workers in the construction industry.

All officially registered jobsites have a corresponding officially registered labor-only company associated with the project. The labor-only companies include government labor markets and private (registered) labor contractors.[17] The labor-only companies usually do not deal with workers directly but rather engage one or more large labor contractors to provide workers and materials to complete the job. On large jobs, there can be from three to seven large labor contractors; on smaller jobs, there might only be one or two. Furthermore, there are usually four levels of hierarchy under each labor contractor (see table 2.2 for an example). Each contractor has one or more brigade leaders depending on the size of his workforce. The brigades are often arranged by occupation, although, in some cases, there are a few occupations within one brigade. Each brigade is broken down into teams of workers within the same occupation usually based on place of origin (province or city). Teams are then broken down further into gangs, and gangs are broken down into work groups. This is the typical structure of the workforce on a larger jobsite for construction projects such as a new apartment complex, commercial real estate, or a subway or transportation project. If the job is a small project such as a home renovation or small business remodel, the workers might constitute a single gang or work group led by a small contractor.

Table 2.2. The organization of electricians from Sichuan on a jobsite

Level	Hierarchical organization (leaders name)	Number of workers at each level
Labor contractor	Zhang	160
Brigade leader	Zhu	60
Team leader	Hong (electricians/Sichuan)	30
	Laing (electricians/Jiangsu)	30
Gang foreman	Du	14
	Liu	18
Work group leader	Lao Gan	5
	DongDong	5
	Chongyi	4
	Li	7
	Zhou	5
	Choi	6

Labor contractors are a central figure in the industry. They can be large, employing hundreds of men, or small, with only four or five men. Some labor contractors are formal, registering with the government, reporting their workers, and paying appropriate taxes and fees; however, most are informal. In some cases, contractors subcontract work out to other brigades or team leaders, and in other cases, they may hire a brigade or team directly. For example, a contractor hired to provide all the labor and materials for a structure (excluding electrical, plumbing, or windows) might not have men trained to do foundational work. In this case, he does not need a full-time gang because he does not normally do this kind of work, so he subcontracts out the work. Alternatively, if the same contractor does not have enough specialized bricklayers or rebar workers, he may hire another team to work with him. In this case, he would hire them for a year and keep them on beyond this particular job. Regardless of whether the labor contractor subcontracts out or hires on a team, gang, or brigade, the organization of workers into groups remains the same. However, as we will see in the following chapters, differences in the employment configuration have significant repercussions for employment relations, labor control, and worker vulnerability.

Beyond contractors, there are two different kinds of workers found in the construction industry: urban *hukou* holders who are employed in skilled positions, and rural *hukou* holders, more commonly known as migrant workers, who perform the manual labor on construction sites. Developers, architectural firms, and general contracting companies have urban *hukou* holders working in the higher-skilled technical and management positions, which represent roughly 20 percent of the industry's employment. For the most part, these workers have full-time permanent stable employment with good wages.[18] On every large jobsite, one can find engineers, managers, and other high-skilled workers from these companies. Qian and Hui (2004, 7) argue that urban "employees" and rural "workers" are not interchangeable groups. Instead, "city-dwelling men and women . . . largely hold management or technical roles and are employed on long-term contracts, unlike rural workers, who are mainly employed on temporary contracts."

All the remaining workers, including leaders and the foremen, are migrant workers.[19] Some are hired by large contractors as temporary workers, properly registered and compensated and given written contracts. These migrants work in the formal sector of the industry and can be found on special projects such as Olympic buildings, on projects held to higher safety standards such as dams or subway construction, power plants, chemical factories, and airports; and on projects that are joint ventures or include foreign investment. Most migrants are hired informally. In some cases, they are hired by the year under informal large contractors but they do not have a written contract and thus face more difficult and dangerous working conditions. Finally, all informal workers under small contractors are usually hired for the duration of the job and paid by the job. These unregistered migrant workers are concentrated in specific sectors of the construction industry: new apartment and mixed-use buildings, smaller commercial ventures, new houses, finishing work, renovations, and repairs. Despite some important differences detailed in the chapters that follow, both registered and unregistered migrant workers remain temporary migrants with little hope of becoming permanent residents in the cities they help build.

The next three chapters explore the lives and work of informal workers, showing how they found their jobs, how they entered the cities, how their work is organized and regulated, and how they become integrated into the cities. Taken together, the three chapters capture the diversity of informal work and show how, for some informal workers, their living and working spaces are blended, albeit in different ways depending on their employment configuration. The next few chapters reveal the city as a city of walls for workers in mediated employment, as a city of villages for workers in embedded employment, and as a city of violence for workers in individualized employment. The chapters show how spatial practices within each employment configuration produce power that shapes not only the politics of informality but also class politics.

Chapter 3

Mediated Employment

A City of Walls

There is no better symbol of China than the Great Wall. Built more than two thousand years ago, it snakes across the northern border and symbolizes the unified Chinese nation. If you were to drive along the section built during the Ming Dynasty, representing about half of the Wall, the distance would be like driving from New York City to San Francisco and back. The Wall's greatness has inspired legends, movies, and even international folklore; it is supposedly one of the only manmade structures visible from the moon.[1]

In the past, the Great Wall played an important role in keeping invaders and nomadic people out of China. Today, the Wall's symbolic significance continues through a famous saying of Chairman Mao, "You're not a real man until you climb the Great Wall" (*Bu dao chang cheng fei hao han*).[2] In this saying, the character for "man" actually has two meanings; it can mean man, or it can mean Chinese, referring to the dominant ethnic group in China.[3] Many migrants in Beijing work in the shadows of the Great Wall, which is about forty kilometers away, yet are unable visit it. Migrant construction worker Zhao lamented this one day, saying, "It's a shame really, I have been coming to Beijing for years but I haven't seen much of the city, and I haven't *even* made it to the Great Wall" (personal interview, December 18, 2004). For Zhao and other migrants, Mao's saying is a cruel reminder that they live and work in Beijing but are precluded from being a part of the city, a part of the *real* "Chinese."

The Great Wall is only one of many walls throughout China. Most major cities have remnants of historical walls surrounding the outer edge of the original city. Government compounds are often surrounded by walls, and today, new housing developments, universities, manufacturing and industrial compounds, and most construction sites are usually surrounded by walls. As you wander cities like Beijing, it becomes apparent that it is a "city of walls." Some of these walls keep people out, and others keep people in; all of them play a role in creating and reinforcing social divisions.

Migrants in informal work under mediated employment live in a city of walls. This chapter explores how construction workers in mediated employment face real and symbolic walls that shape their lives and work. There are two defining characteristics of mediated employment: (1) large labor contractors are the main pathway used to find jobs; and (2) a contracted-labor system regulates employment relations. The chapter begins by examining the labor market. Large informal labor contractors draw workers from a rural labor market, exploiting the rural-urban divide. Then, they re-create this divide within the cities to maintain their workforce. The chapter looks at how the contracted-labor system defines and regulates the employment relationship by merging production and daily reproduction on jobsites where migrants not only work but also live, eat and entertain themselves day in and day out behind the walls that keep them separated from the city. At the same time, this contracted-labor system also spatially separates production (the building process) from social reproduction of labor (creating and raising families) by compelling men to migrate as individuals rather than as members of a family. The chapter also looks at the main mechanisms of control in this contracted-labor system which includes elimination of the exit option, an elaborate scheme of fines to control the labor process and the manipulation of social networks to prevent solidarity among workers.[4] Finally, the last section of the chapter looks at how these arrangements create permanently temporary migrants and the implications.

Climbing Walls: Overcoming Barriers to Migration

Dongzhimen is a new residential construction jobsite. When finished, it will be an apartment complex of three towering twenty-two-story buildings with glittering façades. The first floor will consist of commercial space, and the rest of the building will provide luxurious apartments for Beijing's up-and-coming families. These apartments will cost around US$400,000, well within in the average price range of new apartments in Beijing and a good deal given their prime location near one of the embassy areas and a ten-minute walk to the subway.

In terms of the workers, Dongzhimen is a typical jobsite. In China, over 98 percent of construction workers are peasants who have migrated from rural areas. The vast majority are men, their average age is thirty-three, and roughly 76 percent are married (China Construction Ministry 2004).[5] They have lower levels of educational attainment than most migrants; 70 percent have gone no further than elementary or junior high school. Workers on this jobsite fit these statistics, but a closer look reveals that they are also all unregistered migrants working informally under the employment configuration I call "mediated employment."

It is about eight o'clock in the evening when I walk up to the gate of Dongzhimen. I used to come earlier, but the working hours have been extended. The guard nods me in, and I see Shu Shu, a twenty-four-year-old worker from Sichuan, waiting for me. We walk together toward the dorms with our path lit by flashing lights from welders who are still working.[6] Most workers are already in their dorms when I arrive. There are fourteen men in Shu Shu's dorm room. Pengzi and other men in their twenties and thirties are sitting on a bed, playing cards. Zhou is washing clothing in a basin on the floor, and Gan, who is pushing sixty, is hunched over a book. The activity is concentrated at one end of the room near the only light, while at the other end a few people are lounging around on the beds or sleeping soundly.

Shu Shu, Pengzi, and their friends all found their way to this construction site in Beijing through large informal labor contractors. These contractors are considered "informal" because they are not registered with the government as labor contractors or labor companies.[7] They are large because they usually recruit and hire hundreds or thousands of men, as compared to small contractors who hire fewer than fifty men. Because they hire hundreds of men, they do not have close relationships with most of their workers; instead, they are linked through secondary or more distant social connections. Accordingly, these contractors usually hire gangs or teams rather than individuals. As a result, the team leader and/or gang foremen are the only workers who maintain a close relationship with the contractor.

Peasants use large informal labor contractors to get to the city because doing so offers them solutions to paradoxical migratory pressures that have intensified in the past few decades. In 1978 reforms and the subsequent "economic opening" created opportunities—and increased the pressure—to migrate. At the same time, rising inequality exacerbated the barriers to migration, including high upfront costs, difficulties finding employment in the segregated urban labor market, and the skyrocketing cost of living in the cities.

The pressure to migrate is strong. When I ask construction workers why they come to work in the cities, their answer is almost always the same. Conditions are worse in the countryside, in their hometowns and in the poor provinces. They all talk about the poverty. They tell me that construction work, despite the drawbacks, is much better than rural labor.[8] Most importantly, it opens opportunities to make more money than they made as farmers, stablemen, and grazers. As migrant construction workers, they can pay for their children's education, repair or build new homes, pay for the health care of aging parents, buy a motorcycle, or attract a potential bride.

Economic disparities between the rural and urban have created a significant push for migration. The exact size and nature of the inequality gap is disputed, but most scholars agree that it is large and growing over time and that it is a significant force shaping Chinese society. By 2009, urban incomes were estimated at more than three times rural incomes, representing one of the highest rural-to-urban income ratios in the world (Sicular et al. 2010).

While studies point to "push" factors that compel peasants to leave the rural areas and go to the cities (Zhao 2005), they rarely discuss rural-to-urban inequality as the source of significant barriers to migration. One such barrier, especially for poor peasants who migrate long distances, are the high upfront costs associated with getting to the cities.[9] Upfront costs include a number of potential expenses: transportation, registration, certificates and permits, job deposits, housing deposits, tools of the trade, and safety equipment. Based on my data, I calculate that the average upfront migration cost facing construction workers is the equivalent of approximately 29 percent of the average total annual rural household income.

Once peasants overcome the challenges of getting to the city, they immediately face a second hurdle: trying to find a job in a segmented labor market. As Mingsheng, a construction laborer, states: "I didn't have the money to come to Beijing. Even if I did [come to Beijing], I didn't know anyone here, I wouldn't be able to find a job. It is not possible to find a construction job without a contractor. My Uncle Hu introduced me to contractor Bo who gave me this opportunity" (personal interview, March 12, 2005). Mingsheng's comment highlights both the prohibitive upfront cost of migration and the segregated labor market. If one wants to work in construction, he must know a labor contractor.

A third barrier to migration is the cost of living in the cities and the general foreignness of the urban. The cost of housing, especially rental housing, is well beyond the reach of migrant workers. When they do find cheap informal housing, it is usually located on the city edges, which increases transportation costs. Dong, a steelworker, explains: "In the big cities, the goal is to live as close as possible to your workplace so you don't have to spend hours in the traffic. Our workplace moves from jobsite to jobsite, changing locations. We cannot afford housing near the jobsites, so the best solution is to live on the jobsite" (personal interview, November 23, 2004).

Beyond cost considerations, many migrants do not have friends or family in big cities like Beijing, knowledge of how things work in the city, or backup funds to support them during the tough times. As migrant construction worker Yongli explains: "It is not possible [to find a job on your own]! From the perspective of the company, they don't deal with the peasant workers. The peasant worker's position in society is extremely low; if you come to Beijing without knowing anyone, without a contractor, it is like me going to the United States. I don't know anyone, I don't know anything" (personal interview, July 1, 2005). Yongli's explanation begins by describing labor market segmentation, but he quickly shifts to talking about how "foreign" the big cities on the East Coast seem to migrants from towns and villages in China's hinterlands.

Many migrants who face high upfront migration costs, unstable employment opportunities and high costs of living are unable to get to the cities by themselves. Large informal labor contractors have stepped into this space and instituted a contracted-labor system, acting as a ladder to help migrants climb over an invisible symbolic wall created by the *vast* rural-urban divide.

The Contracted-Labor System

The term "contracted-labor system" is used to specify a labor system that has become integrated into China's broader economic, political, and social system (Hishongwa 1992). The contracted-labor system that has developed in China's construction industry rests upon a standardized, widespread, yet informal agreement (or contract) between migrants and large informal labor contractors. The contractors are not registered, so the agreement is informal and workers are hired informally.

The basic agreement is that the migrant will come to the city and work for a labor contractor for a year, only returning home for two weeks or a month during the New Year holiday. If the contract is renewed, they will return to the city for another year after the holiday break. In return, the contractor pays an agreed-upon salary for the year of work. The contractor pays the upfront costs of migration, which are later subtracted from the worker's salary. The contractor also provides shelter and food. In some cases these are "free"; in other cases, a daily charge is subtracted from the salary. In exchange for a ticket to the city, a secure job, and food and shelter, the migrant worker agrees to forego payment of his salary until the end of the contract. He is paid before returning home for the holiday, with the exception of a small monthly stipend for living costs such as hygiene products and entertainment (soap, cigarettes, cell phone, etc.).[10] These basic tenets of the agreement underlying the contracted-labor system are summarized in table 3.1.

Millions of migrant workers work in construction under this contracted-labor system. Migrant workers agree to these arrangements because it helps them overcome the barriers to migration. It gets them to the city, provides job stability, a lower of cost of living, protection from danger and discrimination, help navigating city life, and a shield from predatory local governments.[11] The contractors also gain from this system. Contractor Zhang explains exactly what they gain as we sit in a trendy Buddhist teahouse sipping tea that costs 370 yuan (roughly US$45)—no less than a week's salary for the average construction worker. He tells me that the most important element of the contracted-labor system is that as time passes, the more he owes his workers. This increases the likelihood that they will stay on the job and minimizes the risk that they will be poached by other contractors.

I point out the obvious, that contractors can decide not to pay workers at the end of the year. In the construction industry, nonpayment and wage theft

Table 3.1. Summary of terms of agreement that is basis for contracted-labor system

Worker	Contractor
Agrees to work full 11 months under contractor	Agrees to pay upfront cost of migration and starting job in city on jobsite (some of which is later subtracted from pay)
Agrees to forgo payment of salary until end of contract (one year)	Gives workers monthly allowance (later subtracted from pay) Provides housing and food (usually on jobsite)

are rampant. Zhang admits that there are "bad contractors" who take the money and run. However, he and many other contractors argue that the nonpayment problem has other, more important, causes.[12] He insists that most large contractors are "real" and want to pay their workers. As another contractor puts it: "We only make money because we have workers. Not paying our workers means we cannot make money in the future. It makes no sense" (personal interview, March 11, 2005). Contractor Zhang points out that recruitment costs contractors time and money; the process is easier, cheaper, and quicker if you have a strong reputation and almost impossible if you don't.

He goes on to explain another less obvious point. Labor contractors insist on hiring workers on a yearlong contract because paying for workers (even during downtimes) is cheaper and easier than letting them go when the work flow slows down and reassembling them when the need arises.[13] He states, "When I need workers, especially skilled workers, so does every other contractor in the city" (personal interview, July 1, 2004).[14] He continues: "This is why we only hire peasants who are in the rural areas. Once they are already in the city, I have nothing to offer them." Peasants already in the city have likely secured housing and developed social networks that help them locate work. On their side, migrants agree to contract labor arrangements because the promise of a year's stable work and a fixed salary eliminates the risks associated with periods of unemployment.[15] Contractor Zhang summarizes: "In reality, contractors have a value and serve a purpose. Thanks to the competition between contractors, the costs of construction have fallen and the quality has risen. In addition, we allow general construction companies to have flexibility in labor use. We make it possible, or easy, for migrants to find and get work. It is obvious that eliminating contractors will fall short of solving the problems" (personal interview, March 1, 2005).[16]

These arrangements challenge the idea that migrant labor is particularly well-suited to the nature of construction industry due to a need for temporary and unskilled labor (Silver 1986; Massey and Phillips 1999). Instead, the contemporary construction industry is shaped by contradictory demand for increased quality at a decreased price, creating the need for a "stable" yet "flexible" workforce. The contracted-labor system makes this possible. These contradictory pressures may help explain the increase in various contracted-labor systems used in construction industries across the globe (Wells and Jason 2010).

Building Walls: Islands in the City Reproducing the Rural-Urban Divide

When migrants arrive in cities, they typically enter into jobsites surrounded by nine-foot walls of corrugated metal that separate the world within from the rest of the city.[17] Pedestrians walk along streets lined by these walls, which are decorated with large posters advertising products and government campaign slogans. Cranes and half-finished buildings jutting into the sky above remind the passersby that there is a construction site on the other side. Most people walk by without a glance, seemingly unaware that behind these walls, hundreds of migrant construction workers live, work, eat, take care of their personal hygiene, entertain themselves, and sleep.[18] For workers in mediated employment, these jobsites are islands in the cities—physically and socially bounded spaces that re-create the rural-urban divide by reinforcing social exclusion, preventing integration, and keeping workers reliant on labor contractors.

Bounded Spaces: Immobility and Control

Migrants live their lives in the cities on jobsites. On the Dongzhimen jobsite, after migrants finish working, they file into the dorms to put away their tools and grab their bowls and chopsticks. They then immediately head for

Fig. 3.1. A jobsite in the middle of the city hidden behind walls. Photo by Marcin Szczepanksi.

the kitchen, stopping at a trough-like sink to wash the grime off their hands and sometimes face before lining up for dinner. After their bowls are filled with soup, each worker grabs a few buns (*mantou*) and scurries to find a place to sit. They sit on homemade benches, squat nearby, or perch on stacks of wood or steel. Members of the same work group or work gang eat together, rarely speaking. After eating, they wash their bowls and chopsticks with cold water and no soap and shake them dry as they return to their rooms.

There are seven dorm buildings. Six of them are similar—two floors with two large rooms to a floor. Rickety metal stairs lead to the second floor and a balcony that follows along the length of the building. The seventh building is different. It is made of nicer materials. The top floor is divided into smaller rooms, each of which is shared by two managers, and the bottom floor contains the kitchen and offices. On the balcony of the workers' dorms, clothes flutter in the breeze, and a few men are bent over small plastic basins, washing clothing or bathing. Inside, the large dorm room is tightly lined

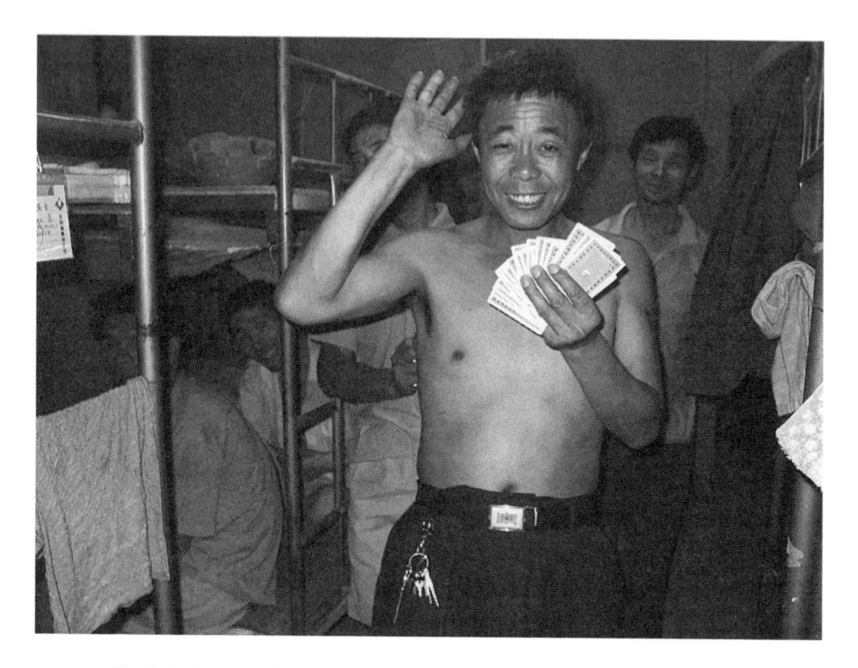

Fig. 3.2. A group of workers in the dorms relaxing after a long day of work. Photo by Marcin Szczepanski.

with metal-framed bunk beds for roughly twenty-six men. The windows have no glass, and the makeshift covering lets in mosquitoes and dust. Beyond this room, an eight-by-five-foot common area opens into another dorm room on the other side. The only electricity is provided by some crude wiring in the middle of the small common area; it runs a hotpot, a television set, and a light. The items were purchased by one of the gang leaders.[19] The uncovered bulb only dimly illuminates the long dorm rooms on each side.

At the foot of each bed, peeping out from under yellow hardhats, hang bags containing each worker's hand tools. The yellow hardhats are more for show than safety. They are made of light plastic that cracks easily, contain nothing inside to protect the head from this hard plastic, and lack straps to secure the hat to the head. The manager's hardhats are white, made of a thicker material, contain a layer of foam inside, and have straps. Company name-badges hang along some of the beds. The badges are issued to each worker, identifying his name, ID number, and the construction company and jobsite where he works. The only other ornaments are the mosquito nets fastened above some of the beds.

Personal belongings are stuffed under the bottom bunks and in the corners of the dorm room. Workers come to the cities with one striped, square plastic bag or duffle bag that contains their personal belongings for the yearlong sojourn. There is no uniform on the jobsite, so they wear whatever clothing they packed. Those familiar with Beijing's harsh winters bring jackets and gloves; others purchase them after they arrive or go without. None of the workers have work boots. The footwear worn on the jobsite includes flipflops, flat slip-ons, sneakers, and Western-style dress shoes. The migrants also bring tools, photographs, books, food, alcohol, canteen bowls, and chopsticks, knives, cell phones, and personal hygiene items such as soap. Some bring idiosyncratic paraphernalia such as small stones or jade pieces, little Buddha statues, special herbal mixtures, or tributes to Mao Zedong. The lack of personal space leads to many conflicts over missing items, so valuables are hidden under mattresses, sewn into pockets, and tucked into other nooks and crannies.

These tightly packed, dimly lit dorm rooms are where these workers spend most of their free time. While the large informal labor contractors are rarely seen on the jobsite, their managers spend their days and nights with the workers, albeit in the nicer dorm building. These arrangements allow managers to easily monitor workers, lengthen working hours, add new shifts, and control what happens during nonworking hours. In sum, the bounded space immobilizes workers and extends managers' control.

Truncated Social Networks

These spatial arrangements also immobilize workers by preventing them from developing social networks in the cities. Most of their interactions are with other construction workers on the same jobsite who are in the same specialty and/or from the same hometown. For example, one work group on Dongzhimen jobsite consist of electricians from Sichuan who work together, play together in the evenings after work, and sleep together in the same dorm room. These men rely on each other for assistance such as loans, sharing of goods such as snacks, phones, and books, help writing and reading letters and the newspaper, help solving problems with other workers and/or managers, moral and emotional support, and advice. Thus, the work groups reinforce indispensible social networks for migrant workers.

As the workers move from jobsite to jobsite, their networks extend across the city and up and down the East Coast, but only among other construction workers, and mostly those from the same hometown or province. These electricians from Sichuan will not have the opportunity to develop relationships with locals or with migrants working in other industries. In other words, their social networks develop horizontally but not vertically. In addition, their networks completely overlap such that the people who form their kinship network are also in their hometown and occupational networks. Because their social networks do not cross into other groups of migrants, they represent strong ties, which are less effective than weak ties in the process of finding job opportunities (Granovetter 1973).

Limited Knowledge and Limited Interaction

These spatial arrangements also reinforce immobility because they prevent workers from accumulating knowledge that is necessary to function in the cities. Many do not know how to use public transportation, cannot find their way around supermarkets, and remain unfamiliar with expected behaviors in public places such as parks and malls.[20] They do not know how to find housing or use the banking system.[21] A striking example occurred one night as I was leaving another jobsite, Dongsishi. It was late, and the last bus had already passed, so I had no option but to take a taxi. Some of the workers escorted me to the street. One of them shouted that he spotted a taxi and then suddenly ran into the middle of the street and stood directly in its path. The taxi driver didn't slow down; instead, he cursed while successfully swerving around the worker. The men were angry, confused, and embarrassed by their inability to flag a cab for me. Situations like this one made it painfully clear how separate these migrants remained from urban life despite living in the cities year after year.

Although both migrants and natives lived and worked in the city, they occupied very different physical and social spaces. Very few interactions took place across these social boundaries, reinforcing the rural-urban divide. No migrant I interviewed who worked under mediated employment had friends, family, or acquaintances who were native to Beijing or urban citizens.

This limited interaction may help explain migrants' and locals' negative perception of each other. Migrants claim that locals are "lazy," which is why peasants have to come to the cities to do all the work. They also see locals as disingenuous. One day at the jobsite, I complained about getting overcharged for a recent purchase. They responded with passionate empathy, each offering their own stories of being cheated by city folks. The workers placed me in the category of "outsider" alongside migrant workers and juxtaposed us to native "swindlers." For me, the experience of being "swindled" was balanced by many other good experiences with local urban residents. In contrast, these migrants had very few interactions with locals, most of which were one-time exchanges that left neutral or negative impressions.

In sum, in mediated employment, migrants climb the wall created by the rural-urban divide and enter the cities with the help of informal labor contractors. At the same time, the urban spatial arrangements build new walls that re-create the rural-urban divide in the cities and keep migrants dependent on the contracted-labor system. Looking inside the walls, we can see how this system regulates employment relations and the labor process.

Inside the Walls: Governing Employment Relations and Regulating the Labor Process

In mediated employment, the most important element of the employment relationship is the withholding of a worker's full salary until the end of the yearlong contract. The longer a migrant works under a contractor, the more expensive it becomes to leave, effectively eliminating an exit option and creating a kind of indentured servitude. However, this system is sustained only as long as workers believe that they will be paid at the end of the year.[22] If a contractor threatens not to pay or earns a reputation of not paying, he will lose credibility, potentially alienating his entire workforce. In this sense, the fates of workers and labor contractors are connected. This connection provides the backdrop for day-to-day struggles over the labor process as workers and labor contractors negotiate the employment relationship. Employers use an elaborate system of fines to control the labor process and shift risk onto workers. In addition, the spatial arrangements of work and social life on the jobsite are designed to manipulate social networks to intensify competition and social divisions among workers.

The Fining System: Monitoring and Shifting Costs

One defining characteristic of a jobsite where workers are hired through mediated employment is an elaborate system of fines. This system is used to regulate day-to-day interactions and produce both self-imposed and top-down monitoring. Workers' pay is docked if they waste material, are injured on the job, cause an accident or injury affecting others, or break the rules of the jobsite (like leaving without permission).[23] Workers and managers carefully keep track of violations resulting in pay deductions and use this information to negotiate their final payment at the end of the year. This system works as an effective control mechanism that raises productivity and shifts costs/risks onto workers.

One day, I was sitting in the Dongzhimen dorm rooms with some workers who had the day off because it was too windy to hang glass on the side of the building. Two more workers entered, one with blood gushing out of his knee. The uninjured worker carefully cleaned and wrapped the wound as he scolded his friend. As they finished, the foreman came in and asked why they weren't working. They made up an excuse and went back to work, intentionally hiding the injury from the boss.

After they left, I asked the remaining workers whether these men would be fined for not using the safety harness that would have prevented the injury. They responded that they were only fined when it resulted in an injury and the manager knew about it.[24] Across multiple jobsites, I found that fines for injuries were only issued when the injury was reported and/or cost the contractor money. As a result, the penalty system did not encourage workers to follow established health and safety regulations but instead shifted the costs of accidents onto workers. In part, this is because pressures to reduce cost and a lack of equipment and training on jobsites discourage worker compliance with health and safety regulations. And in part, workers do not follow health and safety protocols because on a daily basis, managers witness health and safety violations but do not dole out fines for these violations; instead, the penalty system encourages workers to hide their injuries and put their bodies at risk.

This system has pushed the risk of injury onto the workers, a reality that was reinforced one day as I listened to a manager and contractor discuss how much to compensate an injured worker who would be leaving the jobsite, and probably construction, due to the injury. The manager was from the same county as the worker so he was pushing for a higher level of compensation but when the compensation rate reached a certain point, the contractor turned to him and said, "At that price he is cheaper dead than injured." It felt more like a threat than an observation as the room fell silent, negotiations ended and the worker settled.

The penalty system regulates the relationship between jobsite mangers, who work for the labor contractors, and migrant workers. In contrast, social networks are used by contractors and managers to regulate the relationships among workers.

Manipulating Social Networks: Increasing Competition and Preventing Solidarity

In mediated employment, social networks are exploited through spatial arrangements of work and housing that increase competition and reinforce divisions among workers. On the jobsite, men are divided into work groups of five to seven men, all of whom are in the same occupation and from the same province. In many cases, these men are even from the same city, town, or village.[25] In addition to working together, migrants from the same province live together in the same dorm rooms. These arrangements increase minimize interactions among workers from different places, reinforcing place-based networks to increase solidarity within groups and intensify division across groups.

Contractors are well aware of these divisions and the associated tensions. As Foreman Jiang, who currently has men on seven different jobsites in Beijing, explains:

S: Do the men [from different places] live together?

W: They are separated. Otherwise, it would create problems.

S: Generally speaking, what kind of problems? What do they argue about?

W: Their living and eating habits are not the same. For example, let's say that every day you clean your feet but I don't, and we live together. Of course you wouldn't be able to stand it. After time passes, you will always be thinking about this problem, and tensions would arise. On the jobsite, these people are of

> rather low quality; it doesn't matter what you do, it makes them want to fight. (personal interview, January 20, 2005)

Labor contractors suggest that workers' innate qualities, cultural differences, and "low quality" cause most jobsite disputes.[26] This was always the justification given for separating the men based on hometowns and place. However, as I witnessed on the Muxidi jobsite, these disputes and fights are often aggravated by the spatial arrangements of work and housing.[27] Muxidi jobsite is another typical apartment complex construction project in Beijing. One day in April, as I am chatting with Yangbo, a brigade leader, a commotion near the building draws our attention. A fight had erupted between some workers, and within minutes, it expands to include a hundred or more men.[28] Tools become weapons as shovels, hammers, and fists go flying. While I sit frozen with horror, Yangbo jumps up and runs over to Yongli, the foreman. Yongli comes over to tell me that "the police are coming" and that I must leave. I immediately pick up my bag and briskly walk to the gate. The last image I see as I leave is Donghai, a worker I know, with a cut above his eye and blood running down his anguished face.

Days later, I found out that the fight had begun over a wheelbarrow. The cement mixers were using a wheelbarrow that another group claimed was theirs, leaving them with one that was broken. These two groups of workers were from two different provinces, Henan and Shandong. They had had several previous, smaller conflicts in the past. About a week before the fight, a phone and money went missing from a dorm room housing the men from Henan, who immediately accused the Shandong gang of stealing the goods. Since then, relations between the groups had been tense, and the wheelbarrow was the straw that broke the camel's back. Team leaders suggested that eruptions of conflict, though not a daily occurrence, were not unfamiliar on jobsites. Like Foreman Jiang, they explained this as the result of the low character of the migrants and "cultural" differences among the different place-based groups.

Social divisions among migrants increase competition among workers. Place-based networks protect and reinforce occupational boundaries, and, in turn, these place-based groups reinforce and regulate skill acquisition. Skills, skill levels, and skill acquisition are well defined and regulated under the law. Each occupation has a number of skill levels. For example, carpenters have six skill levels, and painters have four. However, on most jobsites, only two levels are commonly recognized for each job: skilled and unskilled.[29] Workers' training and skill acquisition mostly happens through on-the-job training, which is dictated by social networks, as Huzi explained:

S: You guys have different skills. If you want to up your skill level or learn a new skill or occupation, how do you go about it?
W: We all are self-taught workers.
S: What if you go to the company or your boss and request to learn a new skill? What would happen?
W: Each worker individually must raise his skill level or learn new skills. For example, if my skill level is higher them someone else, then I can teach those who are lower.
S: So if you want to learn how to become an electrician, they will teach you?
W: No! They don't like Henan people. (personal interview, December 17, 2004)

Huzi is a bricklayer from Henan. On his jobsite in Xizhimen, all electricians are from Jiangsu. As Huzi points out, there would be no way for him to learn to be an electrician on this jobsite. When a worker wants to improve his skills or learn another trade, he must convince a skilled worker (and the gang foreman) to train him. If Huzi wanted to become a skilled bricklayer, he would need to convince one of the workers in his group to teach him. This would be possible for Huzi because he and the other bricklayers are all from the same hometown. But because the electricians come from Jiangsu, it was inconceivable to Huzi that he might train under one of them. The work and living arrangements of mediated employment thus reinforce divisions among the workers, isolate labor specialties among workers from the same place of origin, and protect occupational boundaries across time and place.[30] These divisions increase competition across and within groups. At this Xizhimen jobsite, Huzi's work group was one of three that worked with bricks. The boss set these groups into competition through incentives. For example, sometimes the group that finished the most work by 4:00 p.m. was allowed to quit early, and at other times, the group that finished first was treated to dinner.[31] In another case, one group who did sloppy work had to take training from the "top" group on their day off. The group conducting the training was given a small bonus at the end of the day; the other group received nothing but the "free training."

In sum, the spatial arrangement of work and housing within jobsites increases competition and reinforces divisions among migrants rather than creates solidarities. Contractors are well aware of these divisions and intentionally exploit them to maintain control over their large labor force on jobsites.

No Walls Needed: Permanently Temporary Migrants

Migrants in mediated employment experience two simultaneous processes that change them from temporary migrants into permanently temporary migrants. First, spending year after year in the city with one short visit home per year destroys families and weakens ties to their villages and the land. Second, being sequestered on jobsites and moving from place to place prevents them from developing new connections in their host communities and putting down roots. Together, these processes create "permanently temporary" migrants, for whom the jobsite becomes their whole life, rendering superfluous the physical walls that contain them.

Migrants in mediated employment enter into the cities under a yearlong contract. Because of the system of withholding pay, they are very likely to stay for the duration of that contract. After their first year, workers return home for a few weeks and then return to the city to complete another yearlong contract. These repeated back-to-back yearlong contracts make it difficult for them to maintain strong connections to their families and hometowns. This is because the structure of mediated employment makes it virtually impossible for them to bring their families to the cities so they migrate as individuals. Children remain in their hometowns, and their wives either remain with the children or migrate for work. In this study, a few husbands and wives had found work in the same city, but most couples ended up in different cities. Even for couples that initially find work in the same city, the construction workers are often moved to another jobsite in a different city after the work ends, so husband and wife are ultimately separated. More importantly, the long hours and hard work that characterize construction jobs make it difficult for men to visit any family members who might be in the same city.

Over time, these arrangements can significantly weaken or destroy family relationships. In this study, a number of construction workers in mediated employment had lost their families as a result of their long-term employment in the cities. Their wives had left or divorced them, or bachelor migrant men had "missed" their opportunity to marry. Their children were raised by grandparents and had little connection to their fathers. For example, Zengzeng, like many others, originally came to the city to make money to build a house for his wife and son. Now, he still returns to the city every year, but his wife has left him and his son is being raised by his parents back in Henan (personal interview, November 26, 2004).

Over time, workers' relationships with and connections to their families, communities, and the land weaken. In the worst cases, the migrant workers stopped returning home and sending money home or significantly reduced the amount they sent. Some of these men felt that they had "lost face," so returning home would result in disgrace. Other men felt betrayed or abandoned by their wives, and yet others did not want to return home because they had failed to send money due to problems they encountered in the city, creating a vicious cycle.

One night in the dorms at Xizhimen jobsite, I ask Gaoshan, a steelworker, about his family. One of the other migrants tells me that Gaoshan works in the city to afford his son's education. Gaoshan proudly adds that his son is in college. I congratulate him, and the others joke that his son is going to college only to end up like his father, a construction worker in the city. This joking acknowledges that even as his father's work as a migrant provides money for the son's education, due to the limitations of the *hukou* system, the main option for even educated rural peasants to earn money is through migration. This reality is shaped by the discriminatory nature of the migratory system, which reinforces the rural-urban divide and prevents migrants from integrating into their host communities. This joke, and others like it, captures a sad irony of mediated employment, in which many migrants hope to help their families overcome barriers, but in the end, their participation only reinforces the system and destroys their families.

Conclusion

Mediated employment has the following characteristics: employers draw workers only from the rural labor market; large contractors serve as the pathway to find work in the cities; employment relations are regulated by an informal but standardized and widespread employment contract; and labor is regulated through limitations placed on mobility, an elaborate fining system, and the spatial organization of the jobsite designed to increase competition and reinforce divisions among workers.

Mediated employment is based on a rural labor market because contractors do not hire migrants already in the city. This is important because mediated employment relies on the rural-urban divide and the inequalities that it creates. Peasants in the rural areas often do not have the resources or knowledge find employment in the cities, where the cost of living is high and work is uncertain. Contractors solve these problems by hiring migrants under a contracted labor system. They pay the cost of migration, give migrants full-time stable employment, and provide basic housing and food in the cities. The safety net created by the contracted-labor system should not be underestimated. Since the system not only provides workers with relatively stable full-time work, but also with housing and food, their daily reproduction is taken care of even in times when there is a lull in the work. These large, informal labor contractors are central actors in mediated employment. They hire hundreds and sometimes thousands of workers. They bring these workers into the cities and move them from jobsite to jobsite and from city to city as necessary. These contractors spend their time networking and bidding on jobs. They are rarely on the jobsites and rarely have strong connections with their workers; instead, they rely heavily on their jobsite managers, the arrangement of production, social reproduction and the production of space.

The contracted-labor system reproduces the rural-urban divide in the cities isolating migrants from the urban world and creating a kind of indentured servitude. Production occurs behind tall walls with guarded gates which prevents migrants from becoming integrated into the cities by truncating the development of their social networks and limiting the knowledge they gain about the urban life. Spatial arrangements of work and social life on the jobsite are designed to increase competition among workers and reinforce social divisions. Finally, this is accompanied by an elaborate system of fines that is used to control the labor process and shift costs onto workers.

In sum, migrants who come into the cities to work in construction under mediated employment find a "city of walls." The first symbolic wall they confront is the "rural-urban" divide, which prevents them from migrating on their own, pushing them into the contracted-labor system that defines mediated employment. These peasants rely on large informal labor contractors to help them climb this wall. Once they get into the cities, migrant construction workers find themselves behind a set of physical walls that surround the jobsite and separate them from the rest of the city. They build the cities, live and work in the cities, but never become a part of the cities. In the end, spending years behind these walls turns them into permanently temporary migrants, fully separated from the rest of society by a symbolic and social barrier stronger than any physical wall. In mediated employment the merging of production and daily social reproduction by having workers live and work on jobsites lowers wages by creating cheaper housing, providing cheaper food and eliminating transportation costs. At the same time, it does provide migrants with a safety net by assuring the daily reproduction of labor through provisions of housing and food. Finally, this contracted-labor system creates "permanently temporary" migrants, disrupting their relationships with people and land in their hometowns and preventing new relationships from developing in the cities, which ruptures the process of social (generational) reproduction of labor.

Chapter 4

Embedded Employment

A City of Villages

Embedded employment is defined by a labor market in which social networks provide the main pathway into jobs and employment relations are regulated by mechanisms evolving from these social networks.[1] Workers in embedded employment are located in migrant enclaves that facilitate the development of these social networks. In 2005, Beijing's local government identified 232 enclaves, or "villages in the city." This term references one way in which the enclaves form: as cities grow, they engulf villages along the edges, and over time, these villages become villages in the city (Gua and Shen 2003). Although this is only one of many ways that enclaves come into being, the term is often used to refer to all migrant enclaves. This is because the term also implies a cultural meaning: enclaves are places within the city that are reminiscent of "backward" villages. The enclaves are central to the lives and work of migrants in embedded employment, so much so that they live in a city of villages.

Migrant enclaves existed before the communist revolution, were eradicated during the era of Maoist China, and have once again become fixtures of the urban landscape.[2] These enclaves are like barnacles, sessile in nature and burrowing into hidden corners of the city, but they also extend tentacles throughout the city that take over neighborhoods and redefine space. There are large and small enclaves in Beijing; the largest hosts more than one hundred thousand migrants (*China Daily* 2005).[3] Altogether, these "villages" house an estimated eight hundred thousand migrants, roughly one-third of Beijing's total migrant population.[4] This is comparable to the estimated 1 million migrant workers, a little over one-third of the city's total migrant population, who live on construction sites.[5]

This chapter explores the relationship between enclaves, social networks, and embedded employment. It starts by briefly touring an enclave to gain a sense of the wide range of activities, occupations, housing arrangements, and social classes that exist in the enclave and help explain the diverse social networks that develop in embedded employment. It also provides a sense that these migrants are not only working in the cities but also living their lives as they establish homes, get married, have children and build new social networks in the cities. This diversity of social networks is unique to this employment configuration. The next section parses out the different types of social networks, how they operate, and what mechanisms are associated with each type. This is followed by two sections presenting embedded employment. One shows how social networks shape the labor market, and the other shows how they regulate employment relations. The last section looks at how workers under this employment configuration are less vulnerable in relation to their contractor but more vulnerable in relation to the state.

A Glimpse into One of Beijing's 232 Villages

Bajiacun, also referred to as Henan village, is one of the enclaves that provide much of the data for this study.[6] It is located in Haidian district on the northwest edge of Beijing, north of the university area. It covers roughly one square mile and includes four sections: Qian Bajia, Hou Bajia, Dashiqiao, and Dongliushu.[7] In 1993, Bajiacun had thirteen thousand inhabitants. Five thousand of these were locals, half of whom had rural *hukous*.[8] The remaining eight thousand were migrants, and 50 to 60 percent of the migrants were registered. By 2004, Bajiacun's population had exploded, reaching more than forty thousand, with the vast majority being migrants.

Shangqinglu, which I nicknamed "the back road," is the enclave's main thoroughfare. It starts near the distinguished Qinghua University in Beijing and juts off in a northwestern direction, leading to the city's edge. The road has been described by more than one person as one of the most chaotic in Beijing. Cars and trucks fight for movement alongside horse-drawn wagons and bikes hauling three-wheeled flatbeds with ten-foot-high stacks of trash. Bicyclists, motorcycles, and mopeds blend with pedestrians, pushcarts, and stray children and animals. There is no clear distinction between lanes or opposite flows of traffic; instead, there is a swarm of people, animals, and vehicles. During rush hour, vehicles slither along in a snarl of traffic, but the road is even more dangerous when the volume ebbs. At these times, speeding cars and motorcycles barrel down the road, barely dodging people and other obstacles in their path.

Vendors demarcate the edges of the road as they form a line on the strips of space between the road and the storefronts. Some sell goods: fruits and vegetables, food from carts, daily necessities (socks, soap, belts, and gloves), used appliances and furniture, used electronics, clothing, and knickknacks. Others sell services: food and drink served at makeshift tables and chairs, outdoor pool tables and card tables for entertainment, shoe repair, and knife

Fig. 4.1. The busy main road down the center of the enclave. Photo by Marcin Szczepanksi.

sharpening. Beyond the street vendors are storefronts providing an even wider array of goods and services: massage, pornography, Internet rooms, restaurants/bars, motorcycle repair, state-owned cigarette stores, tool shops, clothing stores, convenience stores, hair and accessory stores, photography, print and copy services, electronics repair shops, haircuts, and "haircuts," which is code for prostitution services.[9] These storefronts are interrupted by a few indoor markets full of vegetables and livestock and some new buildings housing large spas, high quality restaurants and shiny new Internet and game rooms.

The smells, like the sights, leave an indelible impression. In the fall, the air is crisp, and aromas of cooking waft across the area. In the winter, an acidic odor, caused by the high concentration of open coal used for heat and cooking, burns one's eyes, nose, and throat. The only relief comes in the spring when the dust storms cover the city in a yellow-gray grit carried from the desert plains of Mongolia, dulling both visual and olfactory perception. As the dust settles, the summer arrives, and the smells become pungent again, this time with the putrid stench of public restrooms, which are without plumbing and inadequately maintained. The cycle is completed as the stench is eventually chased out by cool fall breezes.

Fig. 4.2. Construction workers playing pool in the street on a day without work. Photo by Marcin Szczepanksi.

The "back road" serves as the dividing line between different segments of the enclave. On the left, beyond the storefronts, is an expanse of one-story (*pingfang*) shacks and houses. All of the roads going into this side of the enclave are unpaved. Very few are wide enough for vehicles; most are just wide enough for a cart, and some are only footpaths meandering among the buildings. Some of the houses in this area are old and built of brick and mortar while others are newer. The new buildings include both makeshift and more permanent structures. Most homes lack plumbing, which means they share common public water spouts and bathrooms. Many homes also lack electricity or have crude wiring dangling through windows or laying across the floor. Houses are heated with open burning coal that doubles as a stove for cooking. Each dwelling typically consists of one room, which is shared by a family, coworkers, or people from the same hometown.

In contrast, on the right side of the road there is another section consisting mainly of apartment complexes.[10] Some were built during the communist era as state-owned housing while others are new. The older complexes are made of concrete, only six floors high, and lack elevators and other modern luxuries. Each of these apartments has the same layout: a kitchen, living area, two bedrooms, a bathroom, and a balcony. Some of the units have been renovated to include heated water, stoves, washing machines, and flooring; other units are barely more than concrete walls and floors. Each complex has its own courtyard, which is usually covered in communal vegetable gardens and clotheslines. The parking area includes some cars and a few (unregistered) taxis, but mostly motorcycles, mopeds, and bicycles.[11]

The newer apartment complexes are surrounded by a tall wall with guarded gates and entrances. They have no direct connection to the enclaves in that their paved entrances head away from the "back road" toward a thoroughfare with six lanes of traffic, large businesses, and other gated communities. When residents want to enter other parts of the enclave, they have to do so on foot or drive through an alleyway that is hardly fit for vehicles (although that does not stop the traffic). The buildings are colorful with large windows. They climb high into the sky and include elevators, central heating, and cooling and modern plumbing. The courtyard areas have fancy playgrounds and manicured parks, bike racks, and parking areas filled with nice cars.

In all, the enclave consists of these three segments: (1) the poorest migrants who live in the one-floor shacks and houses on the left side of the road;

Fig. 4.3. Migrant workers doing recycling work, which is another important occupation in the enclave. Photo by Marcin Szczepanksi.

(2) the more successful migrants who live across the street and rent out the old communist apartments from locals;[12] and (3) the very successful migrants and Beijingers who live in the newer gated complexes.[13] Bajiacun is a representative enclave in terms of the diversity of wealth and income, occupations and jobs, and experiences in the city. As Ma and Xiang (1998) suggest, this diversity is often overlooked in the literature on China's migrants under the *hukou* system:

> The picture that emerges from some of these studies is of migrants as social pariahs, discriminated against by and excluded from the existing urban institutional environment. They are often seen as poor and uneducated, capable of selling their cheap labour only by taking lowly-paid jobs that are dirty, difficult, dangerous (the so-called 3-D jobs) and tedious, selling vegetables and small household items on the street, or doing repairs and menial work. They are portrayed as the lower class in a supposedly two-class urban society where the long-time residents, with urban *hukou*, are the privileged upper class who enjoys such benefits as guaranteed grain supply, job security, socialist medicine, almost-free housing and heavily subsidized foods and urban services. Such urban entitlements are unavailable to peasants who are depicted as a

> large but implicitly undifferentiated group with little hope of breaking through the hukou barriers. No doubt many peasants in Chinese cities do fit such a picture. However, any attempt to impose such a simplified—albeit neatly dualistic—order on such a complex phenomenon as China's urban society obscures and misrepresents the reality of urban China, masking the migrants' heterogeneous ways of life, diverse employment patterns and income differences. (547–48)

Accordingly, Henan Village challenges notions of migrant enclaves, slums, or ghettos that naturalize images of homogeneous uneducated, unskilled poor migrants living in overcrowded spaces and sharing a subculture distant from the rest of society. The diversity of Henan Village in terms of migrant origins, jobs and occupations, and economic status creates an environment that supports existing social networks and fosters the development of new social networks, both of which shape the lives and work of migrants who work informally in service, retail, and construction.

Building Villages through Many Kinds of Guanxi: Parsing out Types of Social Networks

In embedded employment, social networks are denser and more diverse than in other employment configurations. Parsing out the different kinds of social networks helps us understand why and how this diversity matters. There are at least four different types of social networks, each with distinct underlying principles that guide behavior and distinct mechanisms that regulate social interactions (see table 4.1).[14]

Kinship Networks

Kinship ties and clans are a central organizing unit of Chinese society. Clans are patrilineal ancestral groups that rose during the Sung dynasty (960–1279). They first appeared in eastern and southern parts of China as a result of migration and remain a stronger social institution in these areas today (Greif and Tabellini 2012). They were of central importance in organizing social, economic, and political life. These groups provided public goods and social

Table 4.1. Summary of social networks and associated characteristics

Type of network	Underlying principle	Mechanisms	Short explanation
Kinship	Sentiment and value introjections*	Kinship obligation**	Values established by community and internalized by individuals
Hometown	Utility*** and sentiment	Bounded solidarity	Situational, common adversity, norms of mutual support
Province	Instrumental***	Enforceable trust	Individual compliance with group expectation because of benefits associated with remaining in good standing
Occupational/industry/status	Instrumental (self-interest individual)	Reciprocity and enforceable trust	Individual reciprocity exchanges based on utility

* Value introjection is a mechanism in which the standards and values of a group of people are unconsciously and symbolically made one's own. See also Portes and Sensenbrenner (1993) for more details on distinguishing social networks.
** Peng (2004) explains how kinship solidarity is different from bounded solidarity. The former emerges out of a lineage group, and the solidarity is consolidated by tradition that is practiced across time in relation to family. The latter emerges out of small groups, and the solidarity arises from rationality (when the individual's best interest converges with the group's best interest).
***Both utility and instrumentalism are principles that guide action by weighing costs and benefits. The most important difference is that the former applies this principle to a group, and the latter pertains to the individual.

welfare for members and organized religious services and social activities. They shared property and built ancestral halls, helped with crop protection, loaned money, and provided protection from bandits, overtaxation, and other threats (Rowe 1978). The Communist Party worked hard to eliminate the important role of kinship ties and clans, but they have increased in importance since the economic opening started in 1978.

People who share kinship ties are loyal to the kin group and willing to sacrifice their personal interest for the sake of this larger group. In fact, the values and norms established by the group are internalized by individual members and guide their behavior (Peng 2004). Kinship networks are important because they represent "strong ties," which facilitate trust, responsibility, and obligation. Peng (2004) shows how this trust and obligation reduce transaction costs and reinforce informal institutions. This is particularly important in spaces that have weak markets or that are not governed by formal markets and institutions such as the informal economy.

Kinship and fictive kinship ties are familial ties that extend well beyond the nuclear family to create clans.[15] Although kin groups are a human or cultural universal, fictive kinship ties are not (Brown 1991). Over the course of my fieldwork, I developed my own fictive kinship ties in China. I had friendships with Beijing locals, students, professors, and migrants who lived and worked in the enclave. This included Xiong, a man who fixed bicycles; Lao Du, a man who sharpened knives; and HuaHua, a woman offering hemming and other services using her pedal-operated sewing machine. However, there was one family that sold vegetables with whom I became particularly close. Mrs. Zhang and I ate breakfast, drank coffee, smoked cigarettes, and talked together at least a few mornings a week. I often watched her vegetable stand while she took breaks or went to meet her husband. She cooked dinner for me on a regular basis, and I let her use my shower.[16] If I was out working and someone came looking for me, people told them to talk to her. She knew when I left and when I was due back home. Eventually, I stopped calling her Mrs. Zhang and started calling her *jiejie* (older sister), and she started calling me *meimei* (younger sister). Ever since my time living in Beijing, she has become my closest friend in China. I adopted her family, and they adopted me and my family. This relationship provided me with an understanding of the fictive kinship designations that were so common among migrants.[17]

The Power of Place: Hometown and Provincial Networks

Place-based networks are also a powerful organizing mechanism among migrant workers.[18] There are two different kinds of place-based social networks: hometown and provincial. Hometown networks are probably the most powerful social networks operating in China because they incorporate characteristics of both kinship and provincial networks. They are larger than kinship networks, often encompassing them, but have fewer degrees of separation than provincial networks. Like kinship networks, hometown networks develop based on a common identity, and the underlying principles guiding action include sentiment and values other than self-interest. At the same time, hometown networks are dense: they are both vertical and horizontal, and they consist of both strong and weak ties, making them excellent sources of information and influence.[19]

Hometown networks create social capital through a mechanism called bounded solidarity. Bounded solidarity develops based on a common identity that makes people willing to act in the best interest of the group, even when the action is not necessarily in their own best interest. There is an "enforceable trust" within the group, meaning that individuals face consequences when they do not follow established norms. Bounded solidarity is common in informal lending institutions built upon hometown networks. Some of these lending institutions are more formalized, with standard loan terms and practices, and others are much less formal. For example, Mr. Zhang was one of the people responsible for loans within his kinship group from Shandong province. This group of men met at least once a month, or when there was a need, to hear cases for loans from people who were not only from the same hometown but also a part of this particular kinship group. They would decide who would receive a loan, but the terms and conditions were standardized and applied to most without exception. A less formal example is Contractor Fuguo, who needed a loan to start his business and turned to his hometown network. It is impossible for migrants like him to get a loan through a bank, and though some migrants borrow from family, Fuguo's had recently purchased a taxi for his older brother. He instead turned to his friends from his hometown for a loan, and they were happy to oblige because they knew that if he failed to pay them back, they could exert pressure through mutual friends or call his family. Because of the dense connections in hometown networks, Fuguo's family members would feel obligated to pay the loan even if he could not. Failing to fulfill the loan obligation could make their life in the village difficult or even result in vengeful acts against Fuguo, his family, or his friends. Thus, informal lending institutions supported by hometown networks function well because they are regulated by enforceable trust.

Provincial networks are quite different from hometown networks even though they are both place-based. Provincial networks take on significance only after migrants leave their province and are associated with what is known as "place-based ethnicity," a concept that helps us understand how a seemingly homogeneous population constructs and maintains strong solidarities and divisions (Honig 1992).[20] It is difficult to think of the Chinese as having different "ethnicities." When I arrived in China for my first language-training program, I wandered the streets of Beijing, overwhelmed by what I saw as undifferentiated mass of people. In the eye of an outsider, in my eyes, all Chinese people were of the same ethnicity, Han Chinese. A few years later, however, this had changed. At a Lantern Festival celebration in a park, my landlord's daughter turned to me and said: "Those people we just passed are migrants. Could you tell?"[21] As I replied, "Of course," I consciously realized for the first time that as I passed people on the streets, I was subconsciously categorizing each person as a migrant or a Beijinger. Chinese can tell between migrants and locals by the way they dress and their actions, but there are other less subtle signals as well: accents, mannerisms, loudness or harshness in the way they talk, their manner of dress, and the work they do. Furthermore, people from different provinces are associated with a host of characteristics and stereotypes attributed to their provincial culture. For example, according to popular knowledge in Beijing, people from Sichuan like hot food, people from Xinjiang are sly, people from Shanghai are arrogant, and people from Zhejiang are good at making money. As I integrated into life in Beijing, I gained a sense of place-based ethnicity that I subconsciously participated in creating and reinforcing.

Another important difference between provincial and hometown networks is that the underlying principle guiding action is instrumental rather than sentimental. This means that in provincial networks, individuals decide how to act by weighing costs and benefits. They comply with group expectations because of the benefits associated with remaining in good standing. Furthermore, in provincial networks, enforceable trust can emerge as a mechanism to assure compliance. However, these provincial networks are so large and dispersed that action is usually based on instrumentality and rarely on solidarity. They are also the source of divisions as well as solidarities. For example, migrant enclaves are often organized along the lines of place-based ethnicity and named after the sending province of the majority of the inhabitants, such as Zhejiang village, Xinjiang village, Henan village, and Anhui village (Honig 1992; Ma and Xiang 1998).[22] This social organization reinforces divisions among migrants from different places but increases solidarity among migrants from the same place.

Status-Based Social Networks

Migrants in embedded employment who live in the enclaves develop new social networks that complement their existing social networks. Existing networks include kinship and hometown networks; new networks, or networks that gain importance in the city, include provincial network and status-based networks, such as occupational networks.[23] In most cases, status-based social networks are large networks with low density.[24] Many are characterized by weak social ties that are both vertical and horizontal. This makes them very good at distributing information but less effective in exerting influence. In these types of social networks, behavior is instrumental, meaning that people act in self-interested ways. The main mechanism guiding interactions in these networks is reciprocity. That is, when one person does a favor for someone else, it is returned. As this process continues, trust and social capital are built among migrants in the network.

In embedded employment, workers have a mix of different types of social networks that are dense, diverse, vertical and horizontal, and weak and strong. In other words, in comparison to mediated employment, these migrants are embedded in many more social networks that connect people with more diverse characteristics. In addition, social networks in embedded employment overlap less than in mediated employment, with each network representing distinct groups of people. These characteristics make them effective mechanisms guiding the labor market and regulating employment relations.

The Labor Market: Combining the Village and the City

Like mediated employment, embedded employment has a recruitment process that involves both contractors and social networks. However, as described in the previous chapter, in mediated employment, the contractors hire hundreds or even thousands of workers, so they usually rely on second-, third-, or even fourth-degree social connections for recruitment. They also hire groups of workers rather than individuals, creating social distance between contractors and workers.

In embedded employment, contractors are smaller, usually hiring fewer than fifty men. More often than not, they use first-degree social networks to recruit workers. Kinship and hometown connections are used to hire peasants from rural areas (in the rural labor market), and provincial and status networks are used to hire migrant workers already live in the city (in the urban labor market). This expanded labor market allows contractors to minimize the burdens of using social networks while creating a flexible workforce and providing workers with options for mobility.

One way that this expanded labor market helps small labor contractors survive is by relieving some of the burdens associated with existing hometown and family-based networks (Menjivar 2000; Guang 2005). For example, Contractor Qi explains that he has an obligation to feed and house workers from his family or hometown, so to lessen the burden, he hires a mix of workers, some of whom are from his hometown and others whom he met in the city (personal interview, April 21, 2005). Qi also hires workers as part of reciprocal exchanges. For example, he hired two workers through Mr. Chu, a local businessman; one is Mr. Chu's friend's son, and the other is Mr. Chu's cousin. In return, Mr. Chu hires Qi for jobs renovating the small businesses and rental housing he owns in and near another enclave.

Contractors also use their diverse social networks to develop a flexible workforce. In the previous chapter, we saw how in mediated employment, a flexible workforce is developed by hiring workers for a year under the contracted-labor system, which gives contractors on-demand access to workers. In embedded employment, contractors cannot afford to do this because they do not have the same levels of working capital to sustain themselves during the slow periods. Instead, they use social networks to hire a mix of workers; some workers come and go as demanded by the ebb and flow of the work, and others are hired temporarily to fill in the gaps when needed. A good example of this is Mr. Ho, a typical small contractor in embedded employment. He recently returned to Beijing after hearing that the upcoming 2008 Olympics was a gold mine for construction contractors.[25] He consciously worked to create a flexible workforce through his hiring practices. He explains that his workers are paid by the job, which means if there is no job, there is no pay. This helps him cope with the seasonal nature of construction in Beijing, where the demand for workers is high in the spring and summer and lower in the fall and winter. To deal with this instability, Mr. Ho hires workers from his hometown who are willing to seek out alternative temporary work when work is slow and return as needed.[26] Daping, Mr. Ho's nephew, is one of these workers. He explains:

W: It is difficult when we don't have work, but we help each other and we have a shared fate.
S: Why don't you find work with someone else?
W: Sometimes I find a job for a few days.
S: No, I mean, why don't you go find a job with someone that gives you steady work?
W: My uncle has helped me and depends on me. I cannot leave him. Also, he is good to me, and he is fair. If I go work for someone else, maybe something bad will happen. Maybe I won't get paid. (personal interview, December 4, 2005)

Daping depends on kinship obligations to protect himself from exploitation.[27] In contrast, migrants Mr. Ho hires from his newer social networks tend to be like Mr. Ma, with whom I had the following exchange.

W: The past is the past! At home I dealt in horses.
S: Okay, so at home you dealt in horses. Why did you change your work?
W: The money is good [in construction]. Also, when I come to find work in the winter, it is easy, not like the springtime when there are so many people looking for work.
S: So, do you return home in the spring?
W: I used to.
S: Okay, what about the future? What kind of work do you want to do?
W: Well, right now I am studying how to drive.
S: So, you want to drive trucks?
W: Yeah, it is really good pay, and if I don't have a job I can change jobs; I can find many jobs if I have a license. (personal interview, December 12, 2004)

Mr. Ho knows that workers like Mr. Ma plan to work in construction temporarily. In our conversations, he lists five others workers who have come and gone in the past year, stating that he intentionally hires a core group of workers who stay and a group who are willing to move on when the work slows.[28]

The diverse and dense social networks in embedded employment also create opportunities for mobility. Workers in this employment configuration are much more likely than workers in mediated employment to change jobs, change occupations, and even move across industries. This mobility is facilitated by their diverse networks. These workers find their way to the cities through hometown and kinship networks, but while they are in the cities, they develop new social networks that complement their existing networks. If work is slow or if they have a problem with their contractor, they draw on these diverse networks to find new work. In other cases, they are more proactive, using these diverse social networks to develop skills and gain experiences that will move them upward.[29]

In sum, the labor market in embedded employment is shaped by social networks. Social networks are the main pathway into employment, and because they are diverse and complementary, social networks minimize burdens for contractors and create a flexible workforce. For workers, they facilitate mobility, making it easier to change employers, occupations and industries as necessary. This is quite different from mediated employment in which workers are recruited to the cities through the contracted-labor system under yearlong contracts that immobilizes workers and stunts the development of their social networks. In other words, in mediated employment, a *lack of connections* prevents workers from changing jobs, whereas in embedded employment, the *diversity and density of connections* allows for mobility.

Employment Relations: It Takes a Village to Raise a Building

Workers in embedded employment are on jobsites that seem to operate without any active management; this is in striking contrast to the constant fining, yelling, threats, and coercion that managers use daily to control workers under mediated employment. Some contractors in embedded employment explain their self-regulating jobsites as the result of an "invisible hand of management"; others attribute it to the fact that they are "good" contractors. In reality, employment relations and the labor process are actively regulated by workers themselves through mechanisms evolving from social networks. In other words, in this employment configuration, the building process is guided by social networks and their associated mechanisms, which develop in the "villages in a city."

Mr. Wu's jobsites provide typical examples of workers' self-regulation. Mr. Wu is considered a large contractor in embedded employment because he has almost fifty men working for him. Sometimes he subcontracts jobs from large contractors whose workers are in embedded employment, and at other times he does finishing work. He is currently competing for finishing jobs at an apartment complex with three buildings.[30] Finishing work includes all interior work such as doors and knobs, flooring (carpet, tile, wood, and laminate), wall coatings (paint, wallpaper, and paneling), trim, sinks, toilets, cabinets, and lighting. Mr. Wu and fifteen competing contractors set up "offices" in vacant unsold apartments. His office is a handmade sign posted in the window and a front room with a desk, hot water pot, and stacks of trade books filled with product options.[31] Buyers visit the offices to choose a contractor to customize the interior of their new apartment.

Mr. Wu divided his workers into four teams that work on different apartments. I enter one of the apartments, and the workers barely glance at me. There is a chemical stench from the work. Two men are in the kitchen laying tile, two more are in bathroom, and a few others are laying laminate wood flooring in the rest of the apartment. When I walk in they ignore me and continue working throughout my whole visit without taking a break. These men work at a furious pace, and they work late. Sometimes I stop in around 10:00 p.m. on my way home from the dorms of another jobsite, and I find them still working. This tenacious industriousness provides a jarring comparison to the work process in mediated employment in which workers use my arrival as an excuse to slow down or to take a break; only do limited overtime and demand overtime pay; and set and follow a deliberate slow pace, which results in constant negotiation as managers try to speed up the work.[32]

In embedded employment, what explains the willingness of workers to work at a fast and focused pace and to put in long hours without the carrot of extra pay or the stick of a contractor threatening repercussions? In part, this fast pace of work stemmed from an obvious difference in the pattern of employment: Mr. Wu pays his workers by the job.[33] In theory, this means that the faster they work, the more apartments they finish, and the more money they make.[34] As one worker said to me, "time is money."[35] However, in practice, the work is unsteady, so there is no direct correlation between a faster work pace and more jobs and money. A closer look reveals that the payment system is not the only explanation for why workers in embedded employment work faster, harder, and longer hours.

Their pace of work is also regulated by a mechanism known as "enforceable trust," which arises when an individual member acts in a particular way to stay in "good standing" within their group (Portes 1995).[36] In embedded employment, enforceable trust operates to prevent the free-rider problem colloquially known as "slacking off." When workers are paid per piece, their pay depends only on their own performance, but when they are paid by the job, as they are in this case, their pay depends on other workers as well. For example, one hot evening in June, I stop by Mr. Wu's jobsite. Weiyu, a worker I also knew from the enclave, stops to talk to me. Within a minute, the others begin harassing him, and he quickly excuses himself and returns to painting. Another evening, I watch as the men hang wallpaper, with one man putting on the paste and two hanging the paper. As Little Zhou spreads the paste, the others tease him, "You must be daydreaming about your girlfriend," insinuating that he is working too slowly. During yet other visits, I watch workers compete good-naturedly to finish a floor or wall, with the fastest worker gaining kudos from the others. This kind of self-regulating activity, or "workers regulating workers," is common and helps explain why labor contractors do not have to actively "manage" their workers in embedded employment.[37]

One outcome of the working conditions in embedded employment is worker "burnout." The long hours, fast pace, chemicals, and arduous nature of the work means that these young men cannot stay in the industry for long before it takes a serious toll on their health. In embedded employment, most men are young, whereas in mediated employment, men vary in age. In embedded employment, drug use and other performance enhancers are more prevalent, helping men keep up with the pace of work and long hours but producing greater physical consequences in the long run.

Another outcome of embedded employment is that workers are trained in multiple skills, which provides them with mobility and the contractors with labor flexibility. For example, about half of Mr. Wu's work is on new construction jobsites where the work is subcontracted to him by contractors in mediated employment. He has two teams of workers doing electrical work at a new construction site where the rest of the workers are in mediated employment under other contractors. One of these contractors is Mr. Liu, who has more than three hundred workers spread across four jobsites. Mr. Liu subcontracts work out when he is behind on a project timeline. The workers under Mr. Liu live, sleep, and work on the jobsite. In contrast, Mr. Wu's workers come in the morning and leave in the evening. Furthermore, the workers are spatially separated, with Mr. Wu's men working on building no. 2, and Mr. Liu's men work on buildings no. 4 and 5. These spatial arrangements of work, which often naturally follow the production process in construction, create few opportunities for workers under mediated and embedded employment on the same jobsite to interact.[38]

Mr. Wu does not only encourage cross-training, he requires it. This is because it makes it easier for him to find jobs, especially subcontracted work. His workers are all from the same province, so their language and cultural differences are small, which reinforces the process. This is illustrated by my interview with Cao Wei, a construction worker from the enclave:

S: What kind of work do you do?
W: You name it.
S: I mean on this jobsite?
W: Whatever the boss assigns to me, sometimes painting, sometimes cement work, [sometimes other work].
S: How did you learn all of those different skills?
W: When I started I really didn't know a lot. I could lay brick well. Over time, the others trained me in painting, tiling, and plumbing, things like that.
S: Who gets to decide what and when you will be trained?
W: The boss, you have to do what needs to be done.
S: Do you all get paid the same?
W: Yep, we all get the same pay.[39] (personal interview, March 10, 2005)[40]

As we see in figure 4.4, in embedded employment workers all come from one province, in this case, Hubei. Within this province, they come from different cities, and there is often overlap between hometown and occupations. The plumbers are from one city in the province, and the cement workers come from another city, but they are all from the same province. These workers from the same province are more likely to cross-train. In contrast, in mediated employment, the contractor draws from a number of provinces, and occupations are often divided by province, making it difficult, if not impossible, to institute cross-training.

In mediated employment, provincial divisions prevent cross-training because they are used to police occupational boundaries. For example, one contractor might have cement mixers from Henan, electricians from Sichuan,

Social organization of workgroups in embedded employment

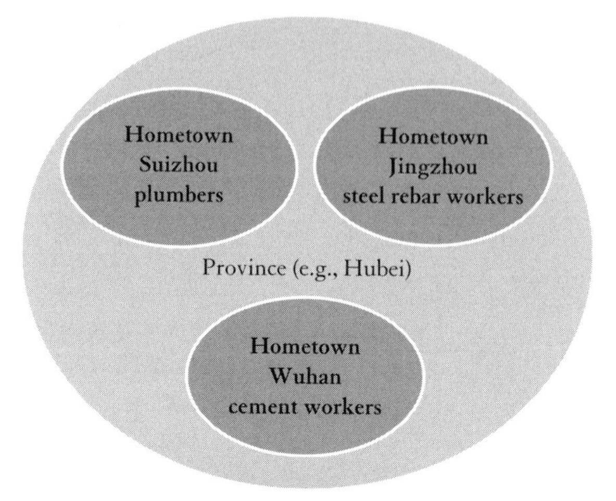

Social organization of workgroups in mediated employment

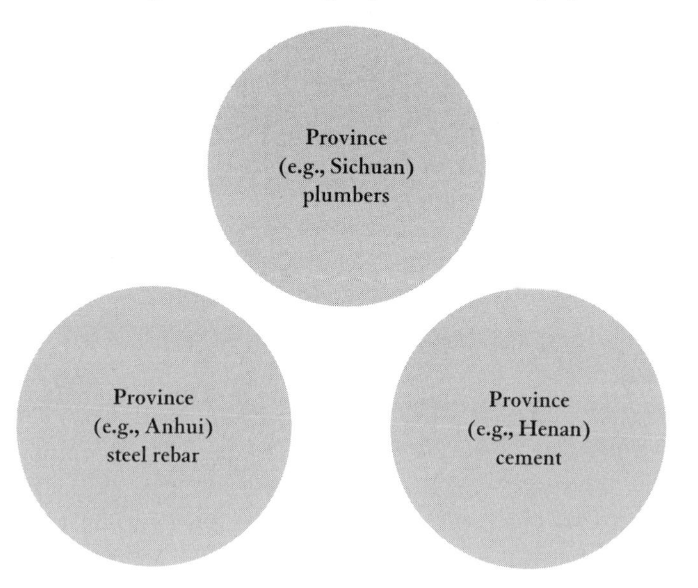

Fig. 4.4. Social organization of workers in mediated and embedded employment.

and steelworkers from Anhui. In the context of these arrangements, it becomes almost impossible for workers to change their occupation because they must get migrants from a difference province to agree and to train them, which rarely happens (see chapter 3).

In sum, place-based social networks operate quite differently across employment configurations. In mediated employment, place-based social networks constrain skill acquisition and occupational mobility. In contrast, in embedded employment, they actually facilitate these processes. The ways that social networks facilitate and constrain skill acquisition captures how, more generally, place-based social networks reinforce divisions among migrants in some cases and help migrants overcome these divisions in other cases.

Precarious Existence: From Sojourner to Settler but Still an Outsider

Migrants in embedded employment follow what is known as the "sojourner to settler" migration model, meaning that they start off by coming into the cities for short stints to make money and then end up settling. They bring their families with them and live in the same city, and often in the same enclave, for years. Over time, they develop friends, families, and sometimes businesses. Their wives and older children work in the enclave or in jobs across the city while their younger children attend migrant schools. They interact with both migrants and locals and develop dense social networks that enhance their social life and their job opportunities. These spatial arrangements allow them to gain knowledge of the city, learn how the local government operates, master the transportation system, and figure out expected behaviors and customs.

However, this "settling" creates contradictions. On the one hand, life in the enclaves increases their connectedness to the city. On the other hand, it makes them visible and vulnerable to state repression. These workers are unregistered temporary migrants, meaning they have no legal right to be in the city. The enclaves are also informal and unregistered, therefore lacking official status. As a result, they are the target of (1) periodic government campaigns and (2) raids and spot checks. The government campaigns often focused on "cleansing" or "reorganizing" enclaves and/or "relocating" the inhabitants. In contrast, the raids and spots check are examples of "sporadic enforcement" of laws which creates protracted vulnerability among these migrants.[41]

Cleansing Campaigns

In Beijing, one of the most well-known enclaves is Zhejiang village, which at its peak, housed nearly one hundred thousand migrants, the majority of whom came from Wenzhou, Zhejiang province. The enclave developed complex systems of commerce, housing, "public" services, and local authority (Zhang 2001). It had more than forty-six housing complexes, water, electricity, schools, markets, health care, and transportation. It also became one of the most important garment production areas in Beijing, housing twenty different wholesale markets and producing more than two hundred thousand wool overcoats and one hundred thousand leather jackets daily (He 2003). Zhejiang has been the target of periodic state "cleansing" campaigns for decades. Dutton (1998) describes an earlier campaign:

> From 8 November 1995 to 10 January 1996, a small army descended upon a southern suburb of Beijing with a "final solution" to deal with problems of illegality there. The place in question was known in local parlance as Zhejiang village because of the high density of Zhejiang residents. The "small army" was all Beijing and all government: 1500 police from fourteen different Beijing units, 1500 armed police from the Beijing number two regiment and 1700 local cadres from the area itself made up this 'strike force', and strike they did. Forcibly evicted were 18,621 people without appropriate residency papers, 9917 houses were demolished and 1645 unlicensed businesses closed. Zhejiang village was demolished and in this act of destruction a warning went out to all illegal 'outsiders'. They were not welcome and would not be tolerated. (147)

As Dutton suggests, the purpose of some cleansing campaigns is to demolish the enclave and send a message to migrants that they are outsiders being evicted from the city. This includes campaigns that came about because of the SARS outbreak in 2003 and those that were part of the preparation for the 2008 Beijing Olympics. Other cleansing campaigns are focused on reconfiguring power relations (Zhang 2001; He 2003). For example, in 1998, three years after the massive campaign to clean up Zhejiang village, the enclave had expanded rather than declined. The area had new hotels, restaurants, entertainment facilities, and a host of other businesses. Large antimigrant campaigns allow the government to reconcile seemingly contradictory goals of growth, their need for control and stability, and their desire to exclude migrants while maintaining legitimacy.

Spot Checks and Raids

Raids and spot checks are the result of sporadically enforced laws specifically targeting migrants. They challenge migrants' right to a livelihood in the city and have become more contentious over time. A "spot check" occurs when government enforcement officials, like the urban public security officers (*chengguan*), stop migrants, check their documents, and issue fines for a wide range of infractions.[42] In many cases, the migrants must pay the fine on the spot or risk being taken into custody to face more significant repercussions. For example, a group of migrant vegetable sellers near the university district were subjected to spot checks. The urban security officers stopped by once or twice a month to issue tickets to the women because they did not have vending licenses. The associated fine was thirty kuai (roughly four dollars) per vendor. When I asked them why the urban security officers didn't come by every day, one of them answered:[43] "The authorities are smart. They know if they fine us every day, we will have to leave because it will make our business unprofitable. If we leave, they lose their source of income. So, they only come twice or three times a month" (personal interview, May 1, 2005).

In comparison to spot checks, which can happen anywhere in the city, raids occur in the enclave where migrants try to create a safe haven in the city. In one year, I witnessed five different raids in the enclave where I lived.[44] The first was just before rush hour. As four or five public security vans came barreling down the road, the people in the street dumped their goods, grabbed their children, left their carts, turned, and ran. The vans kept driving, and people kept running, growing into a mass of frantic people. When the vans stopped, agents jumped out. Most of them ran after migrants and grabbed whomever they could get their hands on while others taped the episode on video cameras. When the vans were filled, they drove off. Mr. Xu, an unregistered migrant living in Bajia, was picked up in one of the raids. He told me later that he had to pay seven hundred yuan, roughly what he earned in a month, to be released. He was lucky because after making a few calls, he had located a *laoxiang* (hometown friend) willing to loan him the money.

In the past, if migrant workers could not pay the "fines," they were sent to detention and deportation camps, where they had to work off the cost of deportation before being sent back to their home village. In 2003, the laws were amended to replace deportation and detention centers with "relief" houses for migrants.[45] However, in practice, migrants are still detained by police when they are unable to pay the "fines." Da Zhong, an unregistered migrant who manages some outdoor pool tables, has been picked up several times. The first time he was sent to a detention camp, the second time they deported him home, and the third time he was detained for four months and had to pay five thousand yuan for his release.[46] The consequences of spot checks and raids include fines, detention, beatings, deportation, and/or other abuses. Many migrants lose their goods or wares during spot checks and raids, making it all the more difficult to survive in the city.

In sum, workers in embedded employment are even more vulnerable in relation to the state than in relation to their employers. Their precarious existence is created through cleansing campaigns and through sporadic enforcement of the laws in the form of raids and spot checks. These state actions create a situation in which migrants can never be permanent settlers in the city. They also serve as a reminder of migrants' second-class citizenship and lack of legal status and recognition in the cities.

Conclusion

In embedded employment migrants are not only working in the cities, they are also living in the cities and building new lives in the cities. In this sense, production, daily reproduction and social reproduction have, to some degree, been relocated to the cities. Although, the *hukou* system complicates the process as it excludes migrants from many social services in the cities, forcing them to create shadow systems or pushing some social reproductive tasks back to their hometowns. For these migrants, the enclaves are the center of their lives; it is where they live, where they raise their families and where they find their jobs, all defined by social networks. Social networks exist among all migrants, but they take on different forms and functions under different employment configurations. In embedded employment, the main pathway into employment is through social networks, and the main regulatory mechanisms emerge from these networks.

Social networks in embedded employment are denser, broader, and more diverse than in other employment configurations. This helps explain why they play such an important role in the labor market and in employment relations. In embedded employment, social networks are a key safety net for migrants. The unstable and seasonal nature of construction work is countered by social networks that facilitate mobility. Workers can easily move across employers, jobs, and industries as well as across the rural/urban divide to deal with lulls in work. For labor contractors, embedded employment allows them to hire extra "temporary" workers from the enclave to help during busy times and move on during the slow season. Furthermore, when migrants in embedded employment face unemployment, they have family and friends in the enclaves who are able to help get by until they find their next job.

Social networks produce mechanisms that regulate the jobsites and employment relations. Specifically, they create conditions in which workers "manage" themselves, eliminating the need for managers who yell, cajole, fine, and coerce. As a result, workers in embedded employment work faster and longer hours than workers in mediated employment. Embedded employment is full of younger men racing to finish the job and move on to the next. It creates working conditions so harsh that men rarely make it to middle age in this employment configuration. Because workers are the creators and enforcers of these harsh working conditions, they do not hold their bosses, the labor contractors, responsible. They do not demand shorter hours, fewer work days, or a more reasonable pace of work. Instead, they develop new skills and move out of the industry quickly. Those who get stuck stay until they cannot work anymore and then move on to other types of work or end up destitute, decrepit, or dead.

Their precarious work is accompanied by a precarious existence. Migrants in embedded employment live, raise families, and often work in enclaves. Social reproduction is complicated by the *hukou* system which denies migrants access to social services and public goods. In response, in some cases they split social reproduction between rural and urban areas and in other cases they create shadow systems in the cities. A good example is education; migrants must choose between paying exorbitant fees to register their children in the city schools, sending their children home to attend inferior rural schools or having them attend informal "migrant schools" in the enclaves. These enclaves and the social services and public goods that they produce are illegal but tolerated. However, as they become larger and more visible, they are more likely to face government cleansing campaigns, which either destroy or reorganize enclaves. Furthermore, the threat of raids and spot checks is ever-present. Migrants are subjected to the possibly of lost goods, fines, physical violence, detention, and even deportation. These state interventions create a significant source of precariousness, increasing the importance of "villages in the city" as havens for these migrants.

Chapter 5

Individual Employment

A City of Violence

Individualized employment is defined by a labor market in which street labor markets are the main pathway to jobs, and employment relations are regulated mainly through violence. In fact, in individualized employment, violence is a common thread woven through migrant worker experiences in the labor market, on the jobsite, and in public spaces.

Feilian is a migrant worker in individualized employment. Feilian is striking for the kindness that seems to glimmer in his eyes. He invites people to sit and talk; he moves out of the way when someone tries to pass. One day, he shares his orange with a fellow worker, which is all he has for lunch. He is tall and slim. His hair is long and unkempt, his fingernails black with dirt, his teeth rotted, and his face deeply tanned and creased. Yet it is his kindness that captures one's attention. One day, I saw him stop a group of children who were hitting a stray dog. Another time, he spent a week calling in favors, scrimping and scraping to restore a discarded pair of shoes to their former glory so he could give them as a gift to a friend whose own shoes were well beyond their shelf life.

I met Feilian in the black labor market. At the age of sixteen he went to Tibet to work in the coal mines. He worked in illegal mines there until an accident killed two of his friends and injured him so that he now walks with a slight limp. Ever since the accident, he has traveled from city to city with all of his belongings in a small bag. In each city, he works for a while before moving on to the next place. He has been to Shanghai, Guangdong, Qingdao, and Chungdu as well as lesser-known cities across China.

Feilian's days and nights are shrouded in violence. In the mornings, he can be found at a local street market where the local urban security officers regularly stop to collect bribes. If the migrant workers fail to produce a few dollars, they receive kicks or jabs to the ribs with a baton. Feilian refuses to give up his hard-earned dollars, so he often endures such beatings.

Feilian's work involves even more violence. He claims that more often than not, employers hit and beat him. Some bosses hit with their hands, but many prefer a stick, a whip, or another instrument. Feilian has been hit with spatulas, shovels, carrying sticks, a leather whip, iron bars, bamboo, a bench, and a stalk of sugarcane. His most harrowing stories come from his work in the mines, but the violence continues on jobsites, in kitchens, and across his different worksites. There is no relief from this violence; when Feilian is not in the street labor market or on the jobsite, he occupies public spaces where he is still vulnerable. People assume he is a bum, vagrant, or criminal and feel justified in treating him as less than human. They kick, hit, steal, harass, and spit on him. Feilian deals with this violence day in and day out, but somehow kindness still glimmers from his eyes and guides his daily interactions.

This chapter looks at individualized employment and the violence that characterizes the lives of the men who work within this employment configuration. The first section examines the labor market in individualized employment. These migrants find work through street labor markets, which are illegal in China; hence, they are called "black labor markets."[1] These markets flourish in China's large cities despite being illegal. The second section shows how street labor markets are linked to employment relations that are similar to unfree labor, as they are regulated by violence and characterized by slave-like working conditions.[2] The final section turns our attention from employment relations to the men's lives off the jobsite, where hypermobility and hypervisibility increase their vulnerability in relation to both the state and local citizens. Taken together, this creates an extremely repressive employment configuration that is often justified by characterizing these migrants not only as outsiders (noncitizens) but also as beggars, vagrants, or criminals (nonworkers).

The Labor Market: Chongwen and Liu Li

In individualized employment, workers go to street labor markets to find work. These are urban labor markets in that workers must come to the cities to participate. They are also markets of last resort, meaning that many who use street labor markets do so because they have been unable to locate employment through any other avenue. There are two different kinds of street markets: "organized markets" and "open markets." Organized markets are run by labor market bosses who regulate the market while open markets are not organized.

Chongwen, one of the many open street labor markets in Beijing, is located near a bus station in front of a hospital on a main street. This is a good location for the workers. The hospital and neighboring stores provide access to bathrooms; a nearby park provides a quiet place to sleep; and the enclave a few streets away is full of vendors selling cheap food and goods. Each day, anywhere between ten and fifty people gather here during the early morning hours to wait for work.

One morning, a car slows down and stops, forcing traffic to weave around it. The workers quickly descend and start bargaining. I overhear a worker listing types of work he has done: cement, carpentry, interior work, cooking. Another person touts his strong physique: "I can lift 30 kilograms all day long. . . . Just look at my stature!" The driver points at two men and tells them to get in. He needs some hauling done. This is only a day job and they negotiate thirty yuan (just under US$4) each. The next day, the workers report that they were only paid twenty yuan (just under US$3).

By 11:00 a.m., the sun shifts in the sky, and hope of finding work fades for those who remain in the market. The workers move from the street to the bus stand to find shelter from the sun. At this point, it is unusual to see more than ten people in the labor market, and it begins to blend into other activities taking place along the busy street. By late afternoon, the bus stop is exposed to the sun, and those who are left move to the side of the store next door. Each person carefully lays newspaper on the ground as protection from

Fig. 5.1. A street labor market in Beijing. Photo by Marcin Szczepanksi.

the dirt and sits next to their bag. These bags are not the typical "migrant" bags, which are larger red, blue, and white plaid plastic sacks. These bags are smaller, the size of a duffle bag. They are not newly purchased for trips to the city but instead weathered by years of use and exposure to outside elements. Clothes, personal items, documents, and papers are stuffed inside the bags, and in some cases, a blanket or large jacket is tied to the outside.[3]

As the day winds down, time passes more slowly, and our conversations entertain and distract us. Their questions expose their naiveté about life outside of China: "How much does a bride cost in the US?," "How do you clean your ears and nose without letting your pinky fingernail grow out?," "Can you help me get a green card for the US?," and "How long does it take by train to get to the US?" I oblige them, and they oblige me, answering my questions, which probably seem equally strange. I ask where people are from, and one tall, lanky man points out each individual and lists where they are from and how long they have been in Beijing, showing familiarity with the others and their journeys. As the sun sets and dusk appears, the migrants leave the market one by one. We spent a full day in the market and only ate an orange and a steamed bun. Hunger pains become distracting. Those who remain are tired, but they do not leave because they have no place to go. In the street markets, days blend into nights, and nights blend into days.

In contrast to Chongwen, Liu Li is an organized street labor market. As I approach Liu Li, I spot a sea of men lining the street and spilling into a large grassy park near a bridge.[4] These organized street labor markets are often near transportation junctions such as train or bus stations, which make the crowds a little less glaring. However, the market is still a curious sight in a city where any gathering of more than a dozen people arouses suspicion, is often declared illegal, and usually leads to dispersal if not arrests.

I hesitantly walk toward the large crowd of men. At first they ignore me, assuming I am a passerby. As soon as I start talking, they react. They quickly surround me, shouting out work rates and what kind of work they can perform. I clarify the situation, letting them know I am not hiring. The fact that I can communicate with them causes more excitement. I cannot see anything but faces. They start shouting all kinds of questions: "Where are you from?," "What are you researching?," "What are you doing here?," and "How long have you been in China?" The cacophony continues, and the crowd grows, reaching six circles deep, burying me in the middle. Hands and bodies are everywhere, tugging on me and touching my hair out of curiosity. I am scared, and I focus on figuring out a way to exit the crowd. Eventually, a man with a Beijing accent pushes through and says that the police had been called; he grabs my arm, drags me out of the crowd, and tells me to leave.[5]

I bring a male friend to my second visit as protection, but my experience is a repeat of the first. My friend and I are quickly separated by the crowd, and once again, I find myself surrounded. My friend yells and gestures that we should leave. As we struggle to get out of the crowd, a fat man pushes his way toward us; surprisingly, the crowd parts to let him through. He turns to me and demands money. Startled, I reply, "Money for what?" He wants me to give him a "fee" for hiring workers from the market. I ask, "What workers?" He turns to my friend, a migrant, and suggests that I picked him up in the market.

The fat man is Pangzi, the market boss. It takes three hours and dinner to convince him that I am a researcher and that the migrant is my friend. Over dinner, he warns me, as everyone else has, that the street labor market is dangerous. He instructs me to call him the next time I come so that he can assure my access and safety. With emphasis, he states, "I am Chinese, I am a Beijing person, and I am powerful."[6]

Every time I come, I find the market full of chaotic activity. Toward the street, the men are attentive, standing and watching the "no parking zone" where potential employers pull up and park. In the back, men are milling around, squatting, sitting, lying down, eating, and playing games.[7] An employer arrives, and the crowd surges in his direction. He heads to find Pangzi, who speaks with him before turning and yelling out workers' names. About ten men are beckoned, and they line up while Pangzi's goons push back the crowd, making sure that Pangzi and his client aren't trampled. The energy and excitement are palpable and reach a level that feels like the crowd could lose control at any moment. This feeling ebbs and flows throughout the day.

The employer inspects the chosen men and turns around. He picks five more men out of the crowd. The lucky five are standing toward the front; other than that, his selection process seems to have no rhyme or reason. The chosen men stand alert and antsy as the employer announces that he is hiring them to move rubble and dirt. The work will take about a week, and he is paying twenty-five yuan a day plus dinner. Two men working for Pangzi escort the workers to a van. As they file along, the employer takes a second look and grabs one of the men out of the line; the rest climb into the van while Pangzi and the employer walk off toward Pangzi's table. I assume that they are finishing the deal.

Liu Li market is a well-oiled machine. Employers choose the migrants they want, negotiate with the labor market boss, and pay the "head fee" and "transport fee."[8] The migrants are loaded into small vans and delivered to jobsites or worksites. When the work is done, the workers are brought back to the market. This process repeats itself all morning. Some employers walk through, picking their own men, and others go directly to Pangzi to allow him to select the men. Some hire one or two "heads," and others hire a dozen or more.[9] Some load the men in their own vehicle; others use the vans waiting on the side of the park. However, not one employer leaves without first negotiating with Pangzi and paying the fees.[10]

Chongwen (open market) and Liu Li (organized market) are typical examples of the two types of street labor markets located throughout China's large cities. Though there are many differences between the markets, the workers who participate in them have much in common. Most participants are men, and most are migrants, although there are also laid-off factory workers in the crowds. Their ages vary, but overall, the average age of the crowd is older than the average age on most jobsites.[11] Finally, compared with workers in other employment configurations, these migrants are more likely to have a mental or physical handicap or a political mark on their record, sometimes referred to as the "three defects."

The differences between the two types of markets are striking. The organized markets are larger and tend to be located near transportation junctions. They are more volatile and operate through an intermediary, the labor market boss. In contrast, the open markets tend to be smaller, located on local streets, less busy, and less chaotic. Everyone knows each other in these markets. Another important characteristic of these street labor markets is that they are plagued with violence. The character of the violence, however, differs in the two markets. In the organized market, violence takes the form of fights. These fights are a daily occurrence and sometimes include weapons. There are fights between migrants, between labor market bosses and migrants, and between migrants and the potential employers. Fights between migrants break out over a wide range of incidents including stolen items, gambling, insults, taking someone's spot, and money.[12] Migrants also fight with the labor market bosses over perceived injustices, but there are limits to how much they can protest. The market bosses are the only "law" that operates in the market. They have an army of men to enforce their rule, and the police come only when summoned by the bosses. Local authorities and police collude with the street market bosses, explaining why the markets can exist and why the police back up labor market bosses when there are disputes.

Some migrants want to avoid fights, so they choose to frequent the open labor markets. This choice does not protect them from violence. Police and public security officers come by unannounced, tell the crowd to scatter, and demand money as "fines" for violations such as loitering. More often than not, this clearing process includes hitting, kicking, and beatings, especially when the workers fail to pay the "fines." The physical assault continues until the workers gather their belongings and scramble away. In most cases, the police return day after day until the street market relocates. Even once the market has moved, the workers are not safe; the violence follows them out of the street labor markets and onto the jobsites, where it is a central feature of employment relations.

Employment Relations: Violence and Unfree Labor

In this employment configuration, employment relations are shaped by extremely unequal power relations in the context of an unregulated despotic market, which leads to unfree labor and slave-like working conditions. This section explores four characteristics that make this labor "slave-like." First, most of the time, these migrants work for food and shelter rather than wages; second, when they do get paid, they are paid a piece rate that requires an inhumane pace of work and long work hours; third, the main control mechanism is violence; and fourth, the work is unstable, which forces migrants to choose between inhumane working conditions or hunger, begging and criminal activity.

The first important characteristic of these employment relations is that compensation, at least in practice, often takes the form of food and shelter rather than wages. Workers negotiate a wage, but because they have no way to enforce payment, they rarely end up getting paid the negotiated price. Often, they do not get paid at all. To minimize the impact of withheld wages, most workers negotiate food and shelter as part of their compensation. When I ask how much they are paid, a common answer is "we work for food and

Fig. 5.2. A worker hauls bricks for this one-day job. Photo by Marcin Szczepanksi.

shelter" (personal interview, March 1, 2005). Jirong, a migrant in the street labor market, describes how this happened to him:

> I wanted to get paid, but the boss wasn't around. He went on a business trip or went home. The others (workers) didn't have this worry because they were subcontracted under team leaders who brought them as a work team. Every day, one of the team leaders arranged the work for me. I wanted money, but I got no support from him since I was not a part of his work team. So I said, "forget it," but the other leaders said, "Wait a while, be patient." So day after day, I waited but before I knew it, I had already been working a month. At that point, I stopped working, but I stayed and waited for the boss. Ten days passed before he returned, but for each of those days, they subtracted from my wages charges for my food and lodging. The boss returned and said, "What do you want? There is no money left, it has all been deducted." I continued to work because I had no money. Working is just a waste. (personal interview, June 4, 2005)[13]

Jirong's story highlights the ways in which bosses take advantage of migrants' vulnerability. They know that migrants from the street labor market have no money, access to social welfare, or stable place to live. However, working for food and shelter is sometimes better than the alternatives, as Yun explains:

> In Baoding, Xushu city, I worked in a brickyard. We worked three months and they still hadn't paid us a cent. He [the boss] said that a sale didn't come through so he couldn't pay us. There isn't any pay until there is a sale. He paid for the cost of food, made sure we ate, but there wasn't any money, especially for serious things. Like if you got hurt, the most he would give you is 100 kuai [US$16], but we kept working. (personal interview, March 3, 2005)

When I asked him why he stayed, he responded:

> He fed us, and he gave us a place to stay. I knew that once I left, it would be difficult. Where would I stay? What would I eat? When would I find the next job? Sometimes I just need a break from these problems. (personal interview, March 30, 2005)

Yun points out that even when workers do not receive the wages they earn, food relieves their hunger, and shelter takes them out of public spaces where they are constantly in danger of harassment, deportation, or death (from exposure). These inducements to keep working sustain a form of unfree labor. These migrants are not wage workers because often they are not paid for their work. Thus, workers frequently describe these employment arrangements as "slave-like." For example, Yonghua said:

> I worked for this boss for a long time like a slave. He had not paid me since I started. I honestly couldn't contain myself and I couldn't endure it any more. At that point, I was owed three thousand yuan [US$375] he only gave me five hundred yuan [US$62 dollars]. He did this because he thinks that we workers cannot fight back. It was so frustrating. (personal interview, April 1, 2005)

Workers compare individualized employment to slavery in reference to both the form of work and the lack of compensation. They are beaten and harassed, forcing them to work long hours at a fast pace. Also, their wages are often withheld, and they have no recourse. In this case, Yonghua had worked in his job for over a year and a half and was forced to walk away with one-sixth of the amount he was owed. Taken together, Jirong's, Yun's, and Jung's stories point to the ways in which their labor is more unfree than free.

Another important characteristic of individualized employment is that the work is compensated at a piece rate and only paid when the job is done. This payment system is problematic for two reasons. First, the piece rate is so low that workers have to work extremely fast and long hours to earn enough for basic survival. Second, they are at a high risk of nonpayment since they are only paid once the work is finished. For example, DaQiang and I worked on a jobsite in Guangzhou as day laborers. The jobsite was relatively new; it was a big hole in the ground with a poured foundation that would eventually become a small shopping mall. At this stage, workers were building the foundation, structure, and false work.[14] An account of one of our typical days follows:

A dump truck drives up to an open gate at the edge of the pit and dumps large cement blocks. The trucks come every hour or so and add to the mountain of blocks. Then a crane-like machine, which is located in the pit, swings its arm around and sets a large bucket in front of the cement blocks. DaQiang (his nickname, which literally means "big force") and I are charged with loading the bucket with cement blocks.[15] Once the bucket is full, the arm swings around to pick up the bucket, swings back to dump the blocks into the pit, and then swings around once again to return the empty bucket to us. We had to load approximately ten buckets for each dump truck of blocks, and at first, each bucket takes about fifteen minutes to fill. We are paid twenty kuai (US$2.80) each for every truckload that we empty. This means we each earn roughly ten kuai (US$1.40) per hour at our fastest pace. I can only keep up this pace for an hour or so, and even DaQiang starts to slow down after a few hours. To make up for his slowing pace, he works longer hours, though I leave in the early afternoon when my legs are wobbly from exhaustion. After taking a nap and eating, I return to the jobsite in the evening with food for DaQiang, who is still working.

This pace of work combined with the arduousness of the tasks and the length of the workday brings on physical exhaustion. This exhaustion increases the likelihood of workplace accidents. Over time, this level of work cannot be sustained. Some workers turn to stimulants to keep up the long hours and work pace. Long hours and fast-paced work coupled with minimal food intake and drug use quickly turns men like DaQiang into shadows of their former selves. Thus, as they age, they are less likely to find work in the street labor markets and forced into finding alternative means to survive.

All week long, when the gang leader stops by in the evenings to calculate our earnings, DaQiang voices concerns about getting paid. On three of the evenings, there is a discrepancy between the amount DaQiang had calculated and the figures the gang leader presents.[16] Like DaQiang, I feel uncertain of whether this gang leader will pay us. I do not feel his same worry because the money does not represent my livelihood, but it seems insane to work so hard for nothing. We are both relieved at the end of the week when the gang leader finally hands us our pay.

A third important characteristic of employment relations in individualized employment is that violence is the main mechanism of control. Physical violence, or the threat of physical violence, is the "stick" used to control workers. Workers describe being beaten for a number of reasons. Yun, a migrant worker from Henan, was beaten for accidentally breaking a piece of glass that was to be installed at a renovation site. Others tell stories of being beaten for not working fast enough, for complaining about the work, and for not following instructions. Violence is also commonly used to reinforce the nonpayment of wages. If workers insist on getting paid, employers simply beat them. Yong nonchalantly mentions getting beaten on a jobsite where he did some plumbing work:

> *W*: I worked about a month over on the west side of town.
> *S*: So when they didn't pay, what happened?
> *W*: They hit me.
> *S*: What do you mean?
> *W*: When I asked for my money, they came over and hit me until I left.
> *S*: Did they eventually pay?
> *W*: No, they never paid up. (personal interview, August 14, 2005)

I ask Yong why he didn't demand to get paid at the end of the day or at the end of the week. He says that they had agreed to daily payment, but then the boss told him to wait until the end of the month when the job was complete. He could have left at the end of the week, but the other workers said the boss would pay, and he had a good feeling about it. However, his feeling was wrong, and when he complained, he was beaten. No one, including other workers, came to his rescue.

Many workers with similar stories anticipated the violence and, instead of arguing, simply walked away. Violence is so common in individualized employment that the workers recount such incidences without anger as just another mundane aspect of their reality. When I express disbelief, they insist that this is a regular part of their work and quickly produce evidence. For example, one day during a discussion about violence, Gan lifted up Bairu's shirt to expose fresh bright-red scars from being whipped on a recent job simply for threatening to leave before the job was finished. Another worker shows me scars near his eye from being hit with an iron bar.

I confirm the regular use of violence over dinner with Datou, a street labor market boss, and two of his repeat customers who hire construction workers. I ask the about this issue, and they openly admit that bosses often hit workers. They rationalize it by suggesting that hitting "these" workers was the only way to get them to work. The labor market boss explained that migrants are "low quality." He says, "They are more like dogs, less like people" (personal interview, November 2, 2005).

The fourth important characteristic of individualized employment is that the work is highly irregular and contingent. The long hours, fast pace, violence, and wage uncertainty create despotic working conditions. However, when this is coupled with job instability, it leads to desperation.[17] Migrants cannot sustain themselves from work found in the street labor markets because it is unstable and contingent. They often have periods in which they must struggle for basic survival and may turn to stealing or begging.[18] This is not the case for formal workers who can fall back on state-sponsored social welfare. Nor is it the case for workers in mediated employment who rely on their contractors or workers in embedded employment who get assistance from social networks. In individualized employment, workers have no safety net. Jirong describes what happened to him after he had two jobs in a row that did not pay followed by a week without work:

> I was driven to desperation. At first, I asked people on the street for money. I was in the Wangfujing area because there are lots of people shopping, and they all have lots of money. I was worried about the authorities detaining me, but I was desperate. After a few hours I had collected very little money. I was desperate, tired, and hungry. Then, a woman dropped her wallet right in front of me. I swooped down, picked it up, stuffed it inside my shirt and then turned around and walked away. It was fate. It had some money, not a lot, but enough for food until I found more work. (personal interview, June 4, 2005)

When I ask Jung what he does when he has no work and is left without money, he is vague, saying he "takes the only road left." In contrast, Liu is much more explicit:

> That place had a train station that was very close, [so] I "chased the train" home. The only clothes I had were on my back. They were my working clothes, and they were black. I cleaned my hair and cleaned myself up as best I could. Then I told people that I had no money and I was trying to go home. There were some sympathetic people; they helped me. It was two days and two nights before I got home from there.[19]

When migrants talk about times they resorted to illegal activities, their shame is palpable as they hang their heads, avoid eye contact, and lower their voices. Most conversations end with similar explanations: stealing and begging are acts of desperation for men trying to meet their most basic needs.

When we consider all four characteristics of individualized employment relations together, it becomes clear that these arrangements create conditions that are similar to unfree labor. These four characteristics are food and shelter provided in lieu of wages; piece rates that forces migrants into an inhuman pace of work; violence as the main mechanism of control; and contingent and unstable work. Migrants' use of the word "slave" to describe their situation is compelling because they receive little to no compensation to work inhumane hours, and these conditions are enforced by beatings. Additionally, these employment relations occur under the constant threat of destitution, hunger, humiliation, detention, and deportation or worse. Perhaps the most daunting aspect of these migrants' existence in urban China is the violence that not only characterizes their experiences in the street labor markets and on jobsites but also permeates their everyday lives.

Off the Jobsite: Hypermobility, Hypervisibility, and Hypervulnerability

Migrants in individualized employment are just as vulnerable off the job as they are on the job. Their vulnerability is, in part, caused by their hypermobility as they move from job to job, street market to street market, and city to city looking for work. This hypermobility creates homelessness that makes it difficult to meet personal hygiene needs, find a safe place to sleep, and protect belongings. Because these homeless migrants often occupy public spaces, they are vulnerable to harassment from local citizens and the state.

Many migrants in individualized employment are hypermobile as a result of circumstances rather than choice. They cover long distances. For example, Liu went to Gansu in the center of the country and then to Tibet in the far West before spending weeks traveling to reach the East Coast cities of Guangzhou and Beijing. He moved from one city to the next because of work. Generally speaking, migrants stay in one place as long as they find work to survive. However, if the work slows down, or if they hear that there are more opportunities in another city, they will move. Also, if the city where they are located is cracking down on migrants, or if they personally experience an increase in harassment from the state or locals, they might move on.

Their contingent work and hypermobility forces them to move in and out of homelessness. Some migrants find enough work in the market to secure a bed in a shared room and others may stay with friends who live in the enclave, but they are the exception. Most of the participants either sleep on the

Fig. 5.3. A worker from the street market finds protection and privacy behind a building under a tree. Photo by Marcin Szczepanksi.

streets or in a makeshift shelter. As Gan, a street market participant, suggests, they sleep wherever they work, and when they don't have work, they sleep wherever they can find a dry spot (personal interview March 1, 2005).

Their lack of a stable home creates a number of challenges, including theft of belongings, difficulty maintaining personal hygiene, and increased visibility associated with vulnerability. Because these migrants do not have stable homes, they are often forced to carry their belongings with them. Keeping an eye on their few possessions, including the little bit of money they have, is a constant job. As Jin mentioned one day:

W: I use my bag as a pillow so that I can sleep.
S: It's comfortable?
W: No, but it is safe. (personal interview, March 12, 2005)

His poignant answer revealed the level of insecurity he faces and how difficult it is for him to protect his meager belongings. Jin also points out that migrants like him don't use banks, so they have to carry their money with them; everyone knows this, so they are always targets of thieves.

Another issue that emerges is personal hygiene. On a daily basis, most people find water to wash in public buildings or public restrooms. However, they often lack hairbrushes, toothbrushes, and soap. These limitations to personal hygiene leave many migrants looking disheveled, with longer hair, dirty feet and fingernails, wrinkled clothing, and missing teeth. Because they are homeless and disheveled, these migrants are often seen as beggars, criminals, and vagrants rather than as productive peasants working in the city.

These migrant workers are the most visible. They spend their days and nights in public spaces. During the day, they are in the street labor markets and at night, they are sleep near bridges, bus stations and in makeshift shelters. In Beijing, as in other large cities, the homeless are inescapable. Usually, they are migrants.[20] The visibility of these migrants increases their vulnerability in relation to both the state and local citizens. Local citizens see them as causing many of the new problems in the cities such as increased crime, overcrowding, stress on public resources, traffic jams, and dirtiness and disorder. In contrast, these migrants see themselves as part of the emerging migrant workforce, and they are upset at how they are treated by city residents. For example, Yonghua told me:

> Beijing people are lazy. They are civilized and have high levels of education, but it is us migrants who come to the city and do all of the work. Even though we do all the work in this city, they still despise us. When we are on the street, they look down on us. We don't bother anyone but they yell at us. They don't think we are human. (personal interview, April 1, 2005)

Violence and harassment is also perpetrated by the local state. Migrants recount numerous encounters with public safety officers in which they were questioned or asked to produce identification and other paperwork. A good ending to the stories is when they just have to pay the officer a bribe. In other cases, migrants talk about being kicked, hit, and warned to stop begging or get off the streets. In the worst cases, these migrants find themselves beaten, detained, sent to work camps, or returned to their hometown. This still occurs despite the fact dentition centers have been "transformed" into social service shelters that are supposed to help vagrants and beggars.[21]

In sum, the biggest problem facing these migrants when they are not on the jobsite or worksite is that the local state and citizens view them as vagrants, beggars, and criminals rather than part of the emerging precarious working poor. Given that they are classified as the former, it becomes very difficult for them to make right claims. Furthermore, both the state and local citizens blame these individuals for their "misfortunes" rather than recognizing the role of macro socioeconomic changes in creating this new hypermobile, hypervulnerable, and highly precarious segment of workers. As such, they do not feel morally burdened to provide assistance in the form of welfare or charity and instead, partake in the violence.

Conclusion: Violence in the Labor Market, on the Jobsite, and Beyond

Migrant workers in individualized employment face the greatest precariousness both on and off the jobsite. They operate in a sociopolitical context that provides them with no social security or social welfare, no legal protections, and little to no charitable assistance. Their fate is left to the whim of the despotic market, and violence emerges as the main organizing principle on and off the jobsite. Their situation occurs in the context of the relentless drive for cheap labor accompanied by the vacuum created by the lack of protection or assistance.

This level of precariousness raises questions about whether this employment configuration represents voluntary or forced labor. At the heart of this question is the common thread of violence that is woven through their labor market experiences, labor relations on the jobsite, and lives off the jobsite. This chapter analyzes these micro acts of violence and shows how they are part of the employment configuration called individualized employment. The evidence suggest that these migrants can and should be considered workers, not vagrants, and that we should apply a macro lens to place their slave-like labor on the wider spectrum of wage-labor in China's urban economy.

In individualized employment, workers are disadvantaged in the labor market. There is a paucity of social networks. These migrants face disadvantages before leaving their homes and lack social networks and social capital to navigate the cities. They also struggle with other prejudices as many of them have mental or physical handicaps, no formal education or skill training, and are older workers. These disadvantages force them onto the labor market of last resort: the street labor market.

In individualized employment, relations are not regulated by the law, social relationships, or the contract system. Instead these workers are subjected to the brutish nature of the market in which the most powerful actor wins. The power relations are extremely unequal, and violence becomes the main force of regulation. Workers toil under slave-like conditions for food and shelter instead of wages and are forced to work inhumane hours at an unsustainable pace. This unfree labor is elicited through giving workers the choice of facing the literal stick on the jobsite or the threat of violence and destitution off the jobsite.

The highly contingent labor market and precarious working conditions create "floaters" as migrants move from city to city and job to job trying to survive. Like workers in mediated employment, they do not put down roots in the cities, nor do they keep ties to their hometowns. However, unlike workers in mediated employment, these workers are not tied to jobsites or contractors. This makes them much more mobile and more vulnerable. In sum, they have no safety net, whether it a formal social welfare system, the safety of walls or the safety of villages.

Finally, and perhaps most importantly, despite the fact that they spend so much time either looking for work or working, they are often seen as vagrants, beggars, and criminals rather than as part of China's emerging precarious workforce. This framing allows the state, employers, and citizens to blame these individuals for their misfortunes rather than seeing the connections between macro changes in the socioeconomic environment and the situation facing these migrants in their daily lives. Furthermore, understanding these migrants as vagrants and criminals rather than as workers makes it easier to justify and naturalize the violence that is used against them. These workers are denied basic rights because they are seen as neither citizens nor workers; instead, they are more commonly viewed as something less than human.

Chapter 6

Protest and Organizing among Informal Workers under Restrictive Regimes

In the face of difficult and dangerous work, a lack of legal standing, and low status in society, informal workers struggle fiercely against exploitation and fight on a daily basis for respect, dignity, and justice. Their forms of protest are highly varied. Some are individual acts of everyday resistance: One worker intentionally breaks his tool, another worker sneaks extra cigarette breaks, yet another refuses to leave the jobsite until he is paid. On a street corner, a day laborer refuses to pay a bribe to the local urban management officers; he has the money in his pocket but chooses to resist knowing that he will suffer blows and kicks from the angry officers. Cai wei, a worker who comes from the same hometown as his contractor, uses moral pressure to negotiate nonmonetary benefits like a free meal and pack of cigarettes at the end of a long day. Workers also engage in collective acts of resistance. On one jobsite, they organize a massive "sickout," and for five days, rotating groups of roughly forty men out of two hundred, all of whom work for the same labor contractor, feign illness and refuse to work. On another jobsite, workers coordinate across four work teams and three guards to pilfer materials and sell them on the open market to supplement their paltry pay.

Other acts require even more organizing with the intention of creating public dramas. This was the case when a group of workers, desperate to get the year's salary owed to them, arranged for two workers to climb cranes and threaten suicide while more than a hundred other workers carried out specific coordinated tasks as part of a jobsite takeover. One group of workers kidnapped the contractor, forced him to his knees with hands tied behind his back, and made him repent publicly before giving him the choice to pay them or face more torture. In other cases, this organizing goes beyond public drama to intentional disruption. This was the case when a group of workers missed almost a week of work to occupy the streets with thousands of other informal migrants protesting the death of a woman from their province. These disruptive protests can include thousands of workers, last for days and even weeks, and garner support from a cross-class, geographically dispersed group of people participating in corresponding online protests. This chapter documents some of the most contentious issues facing informal migrants and explores how related protests either take the form of everyday resistance, "public dramas" or "protests of disruption." In China, informal workers are more likely to turn to these kinds of protest than to join unions or associations, although there are some examples of the latter (Kumar and Li 2007; Hu 2011; Lee and Shen 2011).

There are three characteristics of the Chinese political environment that help us understand why informal workers tend to turn to nonlegal modes of protest action (Y. Cai 2008). First, China is a one-party state that does not conduct popular or direct elections. Ordinary citizens have no access to formal politics, which eliminates this avenue to exert power or influence. Second, while the Chinese government has expanded institutional channels for grievances, especially legal channels including labor tribunals (Gallagher 2006; Lee 2007), informal workers still lack standing, which forecloses this option for them. Finally, China is an authoritarian state that severely limits protest and collective action, and unless their activities are sanctioned by the state, protesters face a significant threat of violent repression.

In this context, informal workers' resistance includes regular and persistent acts of everyday resistance, but it also moves well beyond hidden, quiet, and often individualized forms of protest to incorporate sporadic, visual, dramatic episodes of collective organizing and protest. There are multiple reasons why this is effective and offers protection. First, everyday acts of resistance are too numerous to squash and not threatening in and of themselves. Second, because informal workers' collective resistance is sporadic, the state cannot predict when and where these dramatic eruptions will occur. Third, once these dramatic and highly visible actions gain widespread attention, it becomes difficult for the state to respond through violent repression. This is especially the case when workers are protesting an injustice that gains widespread support through the Internet where the protests are watched by a wider audience. Finally, informal workers usually do not establish formal organizing structures that the state can co-opt.

Another important structural consideration is the merging of labor and locality for many informal workers (Kudva 2009) in which the organization of work combines with the production of space to shape their resistance, protests, and organizing.[1] The concept of employment configuration helps us see these connections by nesting an analysis of production and social reproduction within a spatial analysis of how these workers are (dis)integrated into the cities: in mediated employment, production (urban) and social production (rural) are spatially separated but production and daily reproduction are merged as workers live and work on jobsites hidden behind great walls; in embedded employment, production and social production occur in densely populated enclaves and create social structures like networks that permeate their workspace; and in individualized employment production and social reproduction are both tenuous as they occur in contested public spaces.

In each configuration, the visibility and territoriality of work and reproductive work are constructed differently, and as we will see, this shapes which issues become contentious and workers' responses. In mediated employment, the most salient and contentious issues are wages and power on the jobsite; in embedded and individualized employment, the most contentious issues are related to place and space. In other words, different employment configurations privilege different identities. The next section deals with resistance and collective protest action among informal workers in mediated employment, and the following section presents resistance and collective protest action among workers in embedded and individualized employment.

Challenging Mediated Employment and Precarity

In mediated employment, everyday resistance and collective organizing and protests are commonplace. Struggles are a daily occurrence on the jobsites, where workers resist management control and challenge the terms and pace of their work. In some cases, these struggles are hidden, quiet, and individualized, and in other cases, they are more proactive, collective, visible, and audible. At the same time, there are dramatic eruptions of collective protests over unpaid wages during which workers stage spectacular visual protests. These protests call both employers and the state to task, in some cases, even pushing reforms over how construction is funded, which is the most important structural cause of unpaid wages in the industry.

Acts of Everyday Resistance: Slowdowns, Sickouts, Sabotage, and Stealing

When I ask informal workers in mediated employment about their grievances, none of them complain about the pace of work, even though it is one of the most contentious issues on the jobsite.[2] This is evident the first time I work on one of the jobsites as a cement mixer. Wanting to prove myself, I work as fast as possible. However, instead of being impressed, my team leader pulls me aside and says, "You need to follow us when we are working." He explains that I have thrown off their pace: "We have a system, a way in which we conserve our energy so that we can work the whole day." I am relieved to learn that they intentionally work at a slower pace and happy to follow them, working only when they work and at the same pace.[3] However, the next day, the whole team suffers for my mistake. Because we finished so much work the day before, the foreman increases our workload. Working at the team's normal pace, we are not able to finish by quitting time. Work group after work group finishes their work and files past us to the dorm area, but we continue shoveling. Hunger pangs induced by the smell and sounds of dinner tempt us to speed up, but we keep our slow, rhythmic pace. Finally, an hour and a half past quitting time, our work is complete, and the foreman dismisses us.

In the following weeks, I witness numerous struggles over the pace of work. Lower-level managers (the gang and team leaders) attempt to increase the pace of work, and workers resist. Managers use incentives such as access to better tools, longer break times, and overtime. They also use penalties such as increasing working time (without pay), switching job assignments, and escalating workloads. In turn, the construction workers push back through slowdowns, sickouts, sabotage, and stealing. Slowdowns are when the workers intentionally slow their pace of work. These were usually alternated with sickouts, which are when one or more workers "take the day off." Another common tool is sabotage, which occurs when workers indirectly but intentionally cause slowdowns or temporary work stoppages. For example, the electricians on one jobsite, protesting their increased workload, intentionally create an outage that halts the elevators and brings most of the work to a stop (because most activity is focused on the upper floors of the building).

However, the dynamics completely change as projects near completion; daily struggles subside despite the increase in the pace of work. Yun, a steelworker at Dongzhimen, explains why:

S: Why do you have to work so fast now, and why do you have a heavier workload than before?
W: We are almost done here, [so] we have to work faster.
S: Why?
W: So we finish on time.
S: But, if you don't finish on time that doesn't affect you, does it?
W: Well, we will get paid less if the job isn't finished on time.
S: You mean you will be fined?
W: No. Well, maybe, but I mean that our salary will be less.
S: Oh, you mean at the end of the year when you return home?
W: Yeah. (personal interview, March, 1 2005)[4]

At Dongzhimen, workers were moved onto two twelve-hour shifts, creating continuous progress on the jobsite during the final stage of construction. As Yun suggests, workers acquiesce to increased workloads and the increased pace of work during this stage of a construction project. If they resist, they know (and accept) that this will decrease their salary. This is because profits decrease every day that the project continues beyond deadline, and if they resist the pace, the contractor can rightfully blame the workers for the delays. However, even at the end of a project, workers do not completely capitulate to their bosses.

During "time crunches," the implicit threat of protest is used to push for other demands, especially those dealing with justice or fairness.[5] For example, one work team of glaziers at Dongzhimen is angry about what they believe to be unfair work assignments.[6] Although the glaziers have been complaining for months, it is not until the project deadline is nearing that they pick a day to work at half pace in protest.[7] The following week, they report that their protest was successful, and they are back to working full speed. When I ask why they didn't protest earlier, one man replies, "It wouldn't have had the same effect. Right now, the gang foreman needs the work done quickly so he bends easier." Other issues that workers push for during "crunch time" include accommodations on the jobsite (water sources/electricity), better or different food, and potential bonuses.

In these daily struggles, workers participate in defining the terms and conditions of their employment and their lives in the city under mediated employment. Their protests sometimes take the form of individual acts of resistance, and at other times they take the form of collective and organized action, but their resistance typically does not extend to include all of the workers on one jobsite or on multiple jobsites. However, there are issues that push workers into more sustained organized collective action, most notably, the issue of nonpayment of wages.

Payment, Power, and Protests

Every year, thousands of peasants petition the central government for assistance with their grievances. Most petitions go unanswered (Y. Cai 2008). However, in 2003 the premier, Wen Jiabao, answered the plea of a peasant woman from Sichuan, Mrs. Xiong, who asked that he intervene on behalf of her husband, a construction worker who was owed 2,240 yuan (US$271) from work done the previous year. Wen Jiabao heard her plea, intervened and the wages were paid. Later that year, Mrs. Xiong was crowned the 2003 "Economic Person of the Year" by China Central Television Station (CCTV).[8] This dramatic event was followed by the announcement of a new government campaign to collect the substantial back wages owed to workers, estimated to be about 175.59 billion yuan ($21.21 billion) at the end of 2003.[9] In March of the following year, the government announced that roughly 99 percent of "the total officially recorded payments owed before 2003" had been collected (*China Times* 2004).[10]

The image of Wen Jiabao fighting on behalf of construction workers and the message that the government would no longer tolerate nonpayment of wages was popular knowledge among construction workers.[11] However, the problem of wage arrears continues, as do worker protests and government campaigns and initiatives. In 2005, the government put forth new provisions requiring bonds to be issued by employers for all construction contracts over 10 million yuan (US$1.46 million). In the same year, another pilot program required contractors to deposit migrants' pay directly into bank accounts, and the Beijing government launched a campaign to rid the city of labor contractors altogether. In 2006, in the construction industry alone, unpaid wages were estimated to be 116 billion yuan (US$14.5 billion) (China State Council 2006).[12] In response, amendments to the Criminal Law in 2011 made some cases of withholding wages a crime.[13]

These initiatives give the appearance of a government trying to intervene in the problem, but in reality, government efforts are poorly implemented and enforced. The practice of requiring bonds for construction contracts is still very limited (Deng and Wang 2006), and there is no evidence that direct deposit of pay occurred in any of the pilot cities.[14] Also, since criminalization, only seven cases of malicious wage arrears have gone to sentencing despite the prosecution of more than two hundred cases (Xinhua News, March 7, 2012). Wage arrears remain a major issue for construction workers, as evidenced by their use of both legal and nonlegal modes of political action. There are a growing number of wage arrears labor cases, which, in 2012, totaled more than two hundred thousand cases, 80 percent of which involved construction workers.[15] Also, there are a large but unknown number of workers who use public dramas as collective action to protest unpaid wages. Many of these events are considered as "mass incidents"; their number is increasing and estimated at between 50,000 and 180,000 per year.[16]

Despite government initiatives, wage arrears remain a persistent and cyclical problem for structural reasons. In China, the law requires that all workers be paid on a regular basis, and wages should not be held longer than a month. If wages are not paid in full by the end of each month, wages are considered to be unlawfully in arrears. However, in mediated employment, wage arrears are a fundament part of the agreement between contractors and workers (workers agree to have their wages withheld until the end of the year). As a result, the aggregate amount of wages in arrears builds until the New Year, when the government launches a campaign against wage arrears. Right before the holiday, they happily take credit for collection of most of these wage arrears, when in reality the arrears are resolved because the year-long contracts are completed. Contractors pay off their workers, and most of this "problem" disappears. The remaining amount of uncollected wages represents nonpayment of wages, or wage theft. It is the nonpayment of wages—*not* wage arrears—that upset migrant construction workers and, if widespread enough, threaten to undermine the system.

The nonpayment of wages is endemic in the construction industry. This problem is also caused in part by structural factors. In the popular press, nonpayment of wages is framed as the result of "bad contractors" who do not pay their workers. In reality, numerous factors lead to workers not getting paid, including inexperienced contractors who underbid jobs, the high unexpected costs of additional "fees and fines" associated with new construction projects, and contractors' greed. The most important factor is the underfunding of construction projects.[17] In some cases, the project is initiated by a state-owned enterprise that does not fund the project to completion. In other cases, the state colludes with contractors and developers to underfund projects and displace the risk onto migrant workers. Because workers are not paid until the project is completed, they are the most likely party to go unpaid.[18] Even when projects are properly funded, if there are unexpected costs, they tend to get shifted down the contracting chain to the workers.

Government officials know that a significant portion of the industry operates in mediated employment, in which the contractor hires workers on a yearlong basis but does not pay until the end of the contract. The government is also aware that the industry relies on this system to create a flexible hidden workforce that is central to industry profits. They are also well aware that local governments are complicit in the funding of construction projects.[19] However, infrastructure and development projects are an important driver of urbanization and tool used to buoy the economy, so there is little incentive for the government to disrupt profits in this industry. This helps explain why the government publicly denounces contractors who withhold or fail to pay workers' wages but has not strictly enforced systematic reforms which might end these arrangements.

Public Drama Protest: From Cranes to Gangnam Style

Although national and local governments have been unable or unwilling to seriously tackle the problem of nonpayment of wages, it has become one of the most contentious issues among informal workers in the construction industry, especially those who work in mediated employment.[20] For these workers, nonpayment of wages is one of a very few issues that motivates workers to overcome divisions and collectively protest across different groups and even across jobsites.

Workers distinguish between cases where the government is responsible for nonpayment and cases where the contractor is responsible. In cases where migrant workers believe the state is responsible, they target the government with "indirect" protests. Indirect protests are protests that use the media to draw attention to the dispute and, indirectly, get the state involved and hold it accountable. For example, one group of workers on Zhongkai jobsite in Guangdong did not get paid. The first step they took was to talk to their contractor, Bo, who claimed he had not yet been paid. He actually encouraged his workers to protest and take over the jobsite to demand payment. In this case, two workers climbed cranes and stayed for three days while other migrants sent out text messages to friends across the city asking for help. Eventually the press came, and someone claiming to be a reporter asked questions. The incident didn't make it to the printed pages of a newspaper, but it was resolved with the partial payment of wages.

Indirect protest relies on actions that draw public or media attention (either traditional or social media) to the specific situation by staging a spectacular and visual event. One protest that epitomizes this strategy is a "Gangnam style" dance protest video by construction workers that went viral on the Internet (Boxun.com 2013). Other notable protests include groups dressing up as famous historical characters and others as contemporary cartoon characters to protest in the street (Sina.com 2013). In interviews, workers also reported participating in the following kinds of public drama protests: (1) jobsite takeovers, (2) taking over equipment and climbing cranes, (3) threatening or carrying out threats of suicide (a.k.a "suicide shows"), (4) taking hostages, (5) sabotage resulting in (immediate) architectural/building failure, and (6) petitioning. These public dramas are designed to shine a spotlight on the case and make it more difficult for the state to participate in or condone nonpayment of wages.

These protests have some noteworthy characteristics. First, the issue of nonpayment of wages can, and often does, unite workers and inspire them to protest collectively. The issue is often framed as an issue of injustice and an example of corruption. This framing, along with the indirect form of protest, helps workers overcome divisions on the jobsite. Once a protest action makes it into the media, citizens across the country often chastise the contractors, developers, and local officials for stealing from the migrant workers. Second, although workers publicly "blame" the contractor as they accuse him of not paying their wages, they are in fact targeting the state. The workers know the state is responsible for the withheld wages so they use the publicity garnered by their protests to implicitly call on the state to right the injustice. Third, while these workers are not themselves members of a labor union or organization, they sometimes turn to NGOs or other kinds of labor organizations for assistance. Fourth, these indirect protests are sporadic and draw from a wide repertoire of collective actions, but they can build into sustained collective action. Because they are sporadic, it is almost impossible for the government to prevent these collective actions and protests. Fifth, because these actions are visible and dramatic, it increases the costs and consequences of government repression. As people watch events unfold, most expect the government to side with the vulnerable and exploited and to squash the corruption. If the state uses repression, it risks exacerbating the situation, especially if their actions are viewed as unjust or as sanctioning corruption. Lastly, these protests, while they utilize public drama to garner support and symbolic power, they are not disruptive. In fact, these kinds of public dramas have become part of a broader set of routinized protests that that characterize politics in China today.

In cases where the money is not paid to workers because of unscrupulous contractors, the workers' protests are quite different in that they are more likely to turn to direct protest action and retributive violence. Direct protest often takes the form of migrants working with NGOs or other organizations to file a legal case against the contractor.[21] However, the most common form of direct action is retributive violence. The retributive violence that workers unleash on contractors not only provides a kind of justice but also acts as a deterrent to future nonpayment. All contractors have their own stories of worker violence and retaliation or know of stories through other contractors. One contractor recounts how a group of construction workers found their contractor and took him hostage, stripped him naked, walked him through the streets of the city, and demanded he empty his bank account (which he did). Another contractor tells a story about a friend who was held hostage for days on one of his jobsites until he arranged payment of wages. Two other contractors recount stories of labor contractors who have lost their lives over nonpayment of wages. Contractor Ho suggests that migrant construction workers are a bit uncivilized and that if they are not paid or treated fairly, they are prone to seek retribution through violence. He laments that there is little sympathy for contractors, especially those accused of not paying their workers, so workers can use violence without facing consequences. There are many incentives to encourage contractors to pay workers at the end of the contract because contractors want to protect their reputation to attract and retain workers, but perhaps the strongest deterrent to nonpayment is retributive violence.

In sum, resistance in mediated employment is grounded on the jobsite and worker-based identities. The structure of mediated employment shapes which issues become contentious. Specifically, the contracted-labor system, under which workers are paid a salary at the end of the yearlong contract, makes both the pace of work and the nonpayment of wages contentious issues. Since they are paid a set amount for the year of work, there is no pay incentive to work fast, and since the pay is withheld until the end of the year, there is a high risk of nonpayment of wages. However, their resistance shapes the day-to-day conditions of work and challenges the inherent precarity of the contracted-labor system.

Protest of Disruption: The Right to a Livelihood in the City

In embedded and individualized employment, protests follow a similar pattern with acts of everyday resistance punctuated by sporadic dramatic collective action, but the issues under contention and identities are different, as is the form of protest. In embedded and individualized employment, the most contentious issues are about their presence and occupation of places and spaces, most of which is done outside of the umbrella of state regulation.[22] This is not to say that these workers do not protest or resist on the jobsite. However, resistance on the jobsite tends to be highly individualized. These workers are mobile, so they often use the exit option when mistreated. Workers in embedded employment also attempt to manipulate loyalties and moral obligations created by social networks to make gains while workers in individualized employment are more overtly subversive, stealing, pilfering, and using violence.

Although these workers confront a range of issues on the jobsites, this chapter focuses on their protest off the jobsite. This is because the most contentious issues among workers in individualized and embedded employment are issues focused on space: the right to be in the city and the right to work in the city. This captures the way that their identities as citizens intermingle in different ways with their identity as worker. Their workplaces change often, as do their coworkers, but they tend to spend time together in the same spaces and places off of the jobsite, which creates the opportunity for dramatic and disruptive collective protest.

Noncompliance: Everyday Acts of Resistance

In embedded and individualized employment, the most significant acts of everyday resistance are related to living in the city outside the state's umbrella of protections and regulations. Entering into the cities without registering, and living and working under informal conditions, is itself an act of noncompliance by migrants. This places them outside of state regulation but also in public spaces such as enclaves and street labor markets. Their active noncompliance is a kind of "quiet encroachment," evidenced by the growing number of enclaves and street labor markets and their increasing size. This noncompliance is driven by necessity and calculated rational behavior; there is no benefit gained for compliance. Migrant worker Mr. Lin explained his decision-making process:

> *S*: So why are so many of the migrants living here without a temporary living permit?
>
> *W*: Why would they register? What would we gain?
>
> *S*: There is no benefit to registering in the city?
>
> *W*: Not only is there no benefit, it is not possible. They will require documents that we do not have and cannot get. (personal interview, April 6, 2005)

Here, Mr. Lin points out that it is impossible to meet the legal requirements to register in the city. Even if workers could register, there is no benefit; they would still be temporary migrants without access to most public goods or social welfare. Once migrants come into the city without registering, they also rent housing in enclaves through informal channels. They start businesses without licenses or find informal jobs in which many work and safety regulations are ignored. Workers in embedded employment bring their families to the city, get married, have more children, separate from spouses, and move in with new partners. Much of this happens outside the state's regulatory umbrella. Migrants do not follow state regulations dealing with birth control and the one-child policy; they do not seek state-sanctioned marriage or divorce; and they do not follow laws on child labor or mandatory education. They set up their own schools and seek medical assistance from the local "pharmacist," who dispenses both modern and traditional medicine. This collective noncompliance is taken as a point of pride for migrants. Mr. Qing describes the sense of freedom migrants express through their noncompliance,

> We come to the city and take care of ourselves. We find our housing, feed our families, find work and take care of our children. No one does anything for us. We are not lazy like the Beijingers; we can take care of ourselves. This is because we peasants have had many experiences with extremely difficult circumstances that have taught us how to survive. (personal interview, December 4, 2005)

Many workers like Mr. Qing are proud of their accomplishments in the city. Migrants who have become rich, set up businesses, or gained a position of authority in the enclave are held up as examples of success. But even the most vulnerable workers, those in individualized employment, are proud and point out that being outside of the state's purview creates freedom. They can choose when to work, for whom and in which city. Migrants in individualized employment contrast their freedom in the cities to the problems they faced in their home villages of control from local officials and ostracism due to social transgressions or conflict with neighbors.[23]

Individual acts of noncompliance carry little risk, but collectively, migrants are vulnerable in the city because their presence challenges the state's ability to maintain social control. This makes their right to stay in the city and their right to a livelihood the most contested issues among these informal workers, both of which are struggles over space. Migrants in individualized and embedded employment occupy public spaces. They congregate on the streets in enclaves, around transportation junctions, and in street labor markets. They live, play, and sometimes sleep in enclaves or in streets, parks, and other public spaces. Their growing occupation of this "unregulated space" presents a challenge to the state's legitimacy and control over social stability, and in response local governments have (1) targeted enclaves with cleansing campaigns and redevelopment projects (M. Wang, Lin, and Ning 2013; He 2003), and (2) developed urban management offices and staffed them with urban management officers known as the chengguan who are charged with policing informal activity. From the perspective of migrant workers, state interventions in the enclaves are far less contentious than their interactions with the chengguan. Why?

Struggle over Place: Land Legacies and the Enclaves

China's unique land rights system creates enclaves in which the land is collectively owned by "villagers," but rented out to the burgeoning migrant population. Since migrants are informal renters rather than squatters, they do not develop a sense of entitlement that we might see among squatters in shantytowns, favelas, and other types of urban informal settlements.[24] This is not to say that government cleansing campaigns and redevelopment projects that target enclaves are not contentious. Local villagers who own the land protest against the selling of land without proper consultation or fair compensation. Some migrants who own businesses or who have invested in building development protest to protect their investment or livelihood.[25] However, the informal migrant workers who make up a large percentage of the enclave population are less invested. When asked, they state that they do not care who owns the buildings and land; that they do not care about the compensation packages (because they are not eligible to receive them), and that they do not care about the quality of the urban redevelopment project. When I asked Huang, an informal migrant worker, about a recent demolition, he responds:

> We are peasants and we do not have a Beijing hukou. Our land is in our hometown. We have to protect our land at home. Of course, we are not happy when

> they tear down the urban villages, but we have no choice. We have to find a new place to stay. (personal interview, August 1, 2009)

In a group interview, others similarly explained:

> Changjiang: It is all about the land. Some cities offer urban hukous but [in exchange] we must give up our land [in our hometown]. If we give up our land, we give up everything. In the cities, we are just laborers. But in our hometowns, we are landowners.
>
> Jifa: That's right. Those who protested the demolition, they are villagers who were peasants—peasants turned landlords.
>
> Changjiang: It is no benefit to us outsiders to protest the demolition. It doesn't matter if we rent a room there or here, in both places they charge us a lot of money and we live in shacks. (personal interview, June 16, 2009)

These informal migrant workers complain about the rent costs in the cities, the low quality of housing and the redevelopment projects. However, many are not willing to protest for the right to stay in a specific urban village in a city where they have little sense of entitlement.[26] This may change if redevelopment projects seriously threaten the stock of rental housing without presenting alternatives (Zhang, Zhao, and Tian 2003) as migrants who live in rentals in enclaves represent about a third of all migrants in China; another third or more live in dormitory housing and the final third either live in the workplace (in basements or backrooms) or on the streets.

Struggle over Space: A Right to the City and a Right to a Livelihood

In contrast, migrant workers and most people in general have become passionate in discussions about, and interactions with, the chengguan.[27] The chengguan are a para-police force established in many cities across China.[28] Beijing was the first city to establish a City Urban Management Office in 1997. It was originally staffed with only a few hundred officers, but by 2012 the chengguan had grown to more than six thousand (Human Rights Watch 2012). These officers are responsible for enforcing urban regulations dealing with city sanitation, loitering, landscaping, parking, and other minor issues. Most of their energy, however, is focused on regulating informal activity, especially street vendors. They target migrants, harassing them by sporadically enforcing urban laws and regulations, extracting fees and bribes, and sometimes verbally and physically assaulting them. For migrants in embedded and individualized employment, encounters with the chengguan are their main interaction with the local government. They report being harassed by the chengguan during everyday activities such as riding the subway, frequenting informal businesses in the enclave, and walking down the street. For example, Laofu described the harassment he faced:

> *S*: If you are not registered as a migrant worker in the city, will you have problems?
>
> *W*: We live here on the outskirts of the city so it is not a problem. It is not the city center.
>
> *S*: But sometimes I see the public security officers and the chengguan in the neighborhood.
>
> *W*: Ah, yes, the chengguan. They are corrupt. They cause many problems for migrants in the city. I was just window-shopping, and they stopped to harass me.
>
> *S*: What do you mean? How? What did they do?
>
> *W*: They asked me questions. Then they wanted to see my identification. I showed it to them but they were not satisfied. They were asking me about my work and where I live. I knew they wanted money. They eventually gave me a fine. I negotiated a lower amount by paying them on the spot. (personal interview, February 15, 2005)

The interactions have changed over time as informal migrant workers are increasingly protesting their treatment by the chengguan and local officials (Swider 2014). Migrants refuse to pay bribes and demand the right to be treated with dignity, especially in the face of verbal or physical assaults. They resist the chengguan who tell them to stop selling goods on the street and those who disrupt informal businesses and work, asserting their right to make a living.

When I ask informal construction workers in embedded employment about their participation in protests, they rarely mention collective action on jobsites. They mostly talk about participating in collective protests that are on the streets, with other workers, against the chengguan. For example, one construction worker joined a spontaneous protest and stayed for three days:

S: Why did you get involved with the protest?

W: These chengguan walk around the city harassing migrant workers. If you are from Henan, they will treat you even worse. This guy was from Henan, and they took his food cart. He was just selling food. When he resisted, they beat him. He cried and said that he will have no way to feed his child. They didn't care. They just beat him and took his cart. (personal interview, August 6, 2009)

Another worker, Xiayu, explains his frustration with the local police and chengguan and suggests that that is why he joined protests over the lack of investigation into a suspicious death of another migrant worker. He talks about living in the city but not getting any help from the police and only harassment from the chengguan. This frustration coupled with his hometown and provincial networks brought him into the streets:

S: Why did you travel across the city to protest?

W: She was from the same province, and her hometown was not far from mine. She came to the city to earn money and help her parents and now she is dead. We did it for the parents. (personal interview, June 11, 2012)

Finally, a small contractor explains why, in the past six months, he has responded to two text messages about conflicts with the chengguan by joining other migrants in protests:

> Dangdang: We come to the cities to work. We work hard. We should be treated like humans, not dogs. We should be respected. We are building China. (personal interview, June 19, 2009)

Workers in embedded and individualized employment configurations get involved with protests against the chengguan because they view harassment as an issue of respect, dignity, and justice. They want fair treatment as workers, as business owners, and as residents in the city. They enter into acts of resistance or protest actions either through social networks, especially hometown networks, or in direct response to an incident. In one case, a hometown association actively organized protests against the chengguan. Many of these associations are active, formally structured but unregistered organizations that provide a wide range of services to migrants. In this association, members were involved in an ongoing conflict with the chengguan that escalated over time. Wulin, an informal construction worker who belonged to this hometown association, explained how they were dealing with the problem:

S: So you have had interactions with the chengguan.
W: Of course, but most of the time they are bothering the street vendor.
S: How do they harass the street vendor?
W: They demand money, issues fines, take goods, and often beat us.
S: So what do you do?
W: Well, sometimes we fight back. Now, if we see someone who is fighting with the chengguan, we stop and watch.
S: Why, aren't you afraid that you will have trouble?
W: No, they are already busy giving someone else trouble. We have agreed that when we see this we should stop, so I stop and sometimes scold the chengguan or take pictures if he is beating the migrant.
S: What happens if you do this?
W: This might anger them. They might try to hit me or take my phone. Sometimes they stop, but sometimes they do not. If they continue, I yell to the other hometown migrants and tell them to come and send out texts and tell them to come. (personal interview, July 11, 2009)

During meetings, members of this hometown association discussed the problems that many members, especially street vendors, had with the chengguan. They decided that when the chengguan came around, anyone who was around would stop and watch, creating a crowd of onlookers. If this did not encourage the chengguan to move along, they would take photos, yell at the chengguan, and call or text more people to enlarge the crowd.

Migrants pull others into the protest not only through personal networks and associations but also through social media. By posting information and photos on the Internet, they spread the protest beyond their social networks, which, in some cases, garners support from a wider audience. The use of networks and informal associations, along with support from outsiders via the Internet, helps informal workers organize protests that can grow and be sustained over time. Thus, what begins as a small protest sometimes continues for days and weeks, ultimately including thousands and even tens of thousands of supporters.

The protests that erupted in 2011 in Zengcheng, Guangdong province are one well-known example. The incident was in Xintang town, also known as "Jean City" because this is where the production of jeans is concentrated (Page 2011). However, the scuffle was between a twenty-year-old pregnant girl who was a street vendor and the chengguan; when her husband interjected, he was also beaten. The next day the protest had grown to more than one thousand migrant workers including informal workers from small factories, street vendors, construction workers, and other service workers. The protests continued for several days and included attempts to march and petition the provincial government, burning local offices, and destroying police cars. Yuanzhang and his friend, both migrants from Sichuan who participated in the protests, explained that migrant workers had also come from other provinces to join the protest and that, at the same time, there were sympathy protests breaking out in Sichuan (personal interview, June 12, 2012).

This particular incident has characteristics of a riot and characteristics of a protest, and although some incidents are quite violent, others are much less so. Regardless, protests against the *chengguan* are more likely to be intentionally disruptive to the government, and as a result, they are more likely to be described by the government as riots, violent, mayhem, and disorderly. They are also much more likely to face repression and retaliation. This particular incident was repressed, and it was also highly censored on the Internet as the government worked to prevent the collective action from spreading and worked to reduce the threat of group formation and the possibility of a social movement developing (King, Pan, and Roberts 2013).

Conclusions: From Collective Action and Protest to Social Movement?

Informal workers in China are not powerless. They participate in resistance and protest on a daily basis. However, organizing and collective protest among these informal workers look somewhat different from informal worker organizing in many other places, in part because of the political environment. In China, these informal workers are excluded from formal politics, lack institutional mechanisms for redressing grievances, and face a significant risk of repression. As a result, they have developed a unique pattern of protest that involves everyday acts of resistance punctuated by sporadic, dramatic, visible, and disruptive protest actions.

Collective protests and struggle by informal workers either takes the form of "public dramas" or "protests of disruption." These protest forms are similar in that they both attempt to gain attention from the state and the public. They also both draw on a shared sense of morality and values as they attempt to build and harness symbolic power. However, a crucial difference is that public dramas use techniques, strategies and targets which are within the boundaries of what the state considers acceptable, in the sense that they have become a part of the repertoire of routinized protests that now characterize politics in China. In contrast, protests of disruption intentionally go beyond these boundaries and challenge the system.

Public dramas are often successful in providing immediate gains for workers, but perhaps more importantly, they can mount a serious challenge to some of the underlying structural features of the emerging labor relations system that creates a large informal workforce and shapes their vulnerabilities. In mediated employment, dramatic protests against nonpayment of wages have drawn attention to problems with the contracted-labor system, which rests upon the rural-urban divide. These protests illustrate the role of the state and development policy in exploiting workers, spurring new state solutions that are gradually moving away from going after individual contractors toward systemic reform of the industry.

Protests of disruption use the strategy of disrupting the normal functioning of government or society by shutting down streets, closing off offices and demanding immediate redress outside of normal channels. Protests of disruption shine a light on state repression and corruption in which the privileged prey on the vulnerable. These protests highlight tensions and contradictions in the system. Migrants are expected to be productive residents of the city, but the state makes this impossible by threatening their livelihoods and destroying their living and working spaces. A vicious cycle exists in which the institutions that support the rural-urban divide force migrants to occupy "unregulated urban space" outside of state protection and regulation, but their presence and activities in this space challenge the state's legitimacy. In response, local governments use urban management officers (chengguan) to try to regain control, which has led to increased protests that draw attention to the state's lack of control, which further weakens state legitimacy. As a result, these protests are much more likely to face harsh repression from the state.

Protests among informal workers are threatening to the state for other reasons as well. First, the state, rather than employers, is often the target of these protests. Second, the demands of these workers are universal, sometimes creating intense symbolic power. The Chinese people easily unite behind the idea that not paying migrant construction workers after a year of work is reprehensible. This is also sometimes framed as an example of corruption, which is a hot-button topic in China and more likely to receive attention from local cadres who do not want their malfeasance to gain attention from upper-level authorities (X. Chen 2011). Similarly, protests frame chengguan who beat informal workers and force them to pay bribes as another example of a corrupt and morally bankrupt local government. This kind of framing helps these protests gain support from a wide swath of society that crosses both class and rural-urban divides.

These findings support Lee's argument that "worker subjectivity cannot be reduced to material interests. Equally important are workers' sense of dignity, justice, and their need for recognition. Postsocialist transition in China spawns labor unrest because enormous normative violence has been inflicted on workers" (2007, 15–16). This form of protest, being both public and symbolic, provides leverage for protesters (Chun 2011). Accordingly, these dramatic styles should not be dismissed as fleeting attempts at "attention-grabbing," but rather understood as part of a broader strategy in which marginalized workers utilize symbolic power. Furthermore, the strategy of reaching the state through public protests and the media also creates the potential for the development of widespread cross-group or cross-regional alliances (either workers unite across place or, more commonly, other social groups such as students, middle-class workers, or urban citizens join forces with protesting workers).

Finally, these protests are also truly autonomous. Because they are fluid and not as structured as traditional social movement organizing, there is no structure for the government to infiltrate and use to co-opt or crush the protests. As one worker named Li put it, "Organizations are like a hand and the government is like a glove that slips on the hand and suffocates or controls the movement. If there is no hand, the glove does not work." (personal interview, June 17, 2012). When organizing, these workers rely more on social networks, informal organizations, and shifting leadership.[29]

Despite the existence of a large number of public drama and disruptive protests by informal workers, they do not necessarily constitute a social movement. A social movement would require a relationship between events (Oliver and Myers 2003), and there is no evidence of relationships among these workers' collective social protests. But do these discrete, isolated protests have the potential to form a social movement? I would argue that they do, but they will need physical space in order to do so. In his analysis of how quiet encroachments made up of individualized actions become political and collective, Bayat (1997) argues that sharing physical space is the key ingredient:

> The fact is that these juxtaposed individuals can potentially act together. But acting together requires a medium or network for establishing communication. Illegal immigrants or tax-strikers cannot resist state action unless they begin to deliberately organize themselves, since no medium like space brings them together. . . . Tenants, spectators, vendors, squatters, and the women described above, even though they do not know each other, may act collectively because common space makes it possible for them to recognize their common interests and identity . . . that is, to develop a passive network. What mediates between a passive network and action is a common threat. Once these atomized individuals are confronted by a threat to their gains, their passive network spontaneously turns into an active network and collective action. (17)

In the case of China's informal migrant construction workers, their use of a highly visible protest forms, alongside the use of the Internet and print media, creates a "virtual space" to organize with a much wider group of supporters. Even among this highly dispersed group, this form of activism presents the potential for the recognition of common or overlapping issues and interests, shared but shifting identities and united struggle.

Chapter 7

Informal Precarious Workers, Protests, and Precarious Authoritarianism

First, and foremost, this book documents the work and lives of unregistered migrants who work informally in China' construction industry. It provides a glimpse behind the modern shiny façade of China's fast-growing global cities, showing how these migrant workers are socially and physically excluded from the very cities they build. They are part of a larger army of informal workers in China's burgeoning urban economy, workers who are rendered somewhat invisible and overlooked in both policy and academic circles. This book makes them visible and, in the process, raises important questions about informal work; aspects of China's development strategy, which is reliant upon a specific kind of labor regime; and China's emerging working class and related contentious protest.

The book is organized around a concept, *employment configuration*, in an effort to make sense of the diversity of employment arrangements in China's growing urban informal economy and, more generally, among informal workers worldwide. The concept is more robust than that of informal work, which is simply defined as an absence of formal employment arrangements.

In contrast, the concept of employment configuration differentiates types of informal work based on two characteristics: (1) pathways into employment and (2) mechanisms regulating the employment relationship. It focuses our attention beyond entry into the informal labor market to understand how people in the informal labor market find their jobs, or their "pathways into employment." It rejects the idea that informal work is "unregulated" and categorizes work based on nonstate mechanisms of regulation.

The concept of employment configuration is similar to that of labor regimes, which as Lee (2007) suggests, "is a powerful analytical tool linking state regulations of labor (through legislation on contracts, minimum wage, social insurance collective bargaining, and the like) and the social reproduction of labor power (i.e., means of subsistence, daily and generational reproduction of the capacity to labor) to workplace control and worker' capacity for resistance" (21-2). It expands the idea of labor regimes, however, to consider informal workers, exploring how informal labor is regulated through mechanisms other than the law, and how production, daily reproduction and social reproduction of labor are merged and separated to create different configurations. The concept of employment configuration also couples this analysis of production and social reproduction with a spatial analysis of how these workers are (dis)integrated into the cities, uncovering additional sources of vulnerability and power among informal workers. In the end, this concept provides insights into how China's emerging labor regime, beyond experiencing a shift from a socialist contract to a legal contract regime, is becoming fragmented. Like in many other countries across the globe, this includes a growing segment of informal workers. It also helps "gender" the labor regime by showing how a "cheap" and "flexible" workforce of both men and women which is created through varying configurations of production, daily reproduction, and social reproduction.

Although this book focuses on understanding structure and process, it does not ignore human agency, nor does it imply that human agency is subjugated to structure. Instead, it suggests that we must understand structural changes and underlying processes to contextualize and historicize both human agency and the potential for social change (Friedman, Pickowicz, and Selden 2005). This allows us to see how informal workers are far from powerless as they resist exploitation and protest their precarity. This includes regular and persistent acts of everyday resistance coupled with sporadic visual dramatic episodes of collective organizing and protests. The form and strategies, in some ways unique, are shaped by these employment configurations and the fact that they are informal workers operating under an authoritarian regime.

This chapter summarizes and compares major characteristics of each employment configuration. It highlights how microprocesses operating in each employment configuration are linked to some of the larger structural factors reshaping social class in China; including migration, the *hukou* system, and the introduction of neoliberal capitalism into China. The second section moves us beyond China and compares the three employment configurations introduced in this book to employment arrangements across the globe in different industries. Finally, the last section discusses resistance and protest among these informal workers and argues that we should recognize their place in China's emerging class structure and their potential role in shaping social change.

Summarizing and Comparing Employment Configurations

One of the main goals of this book is to delineate the diversity of working and living conditions among informal migrant construction workers and to bring them back into conversations about employment and labor relations. The concept of employment configuration provides space to explore informal employment relations and how they are regulated, even if not formally by the law.

Each employment configuration is defined by a specific pathway into employment linked with specific mechanisms regulating the employment relationship (see table 7.1). There are three distinct employment configurations among informal construction workers in China: mediated, embedded, and individualized. However, we may find other employment configurations if we expand our research to include formal workers in construction or informal and formal workers in other industries.

In mediated employment, workers find jobs through large contractors, and their employment is regulated by a contracted-labor system. It is a rural labor market because these large contractors only recruit peasants who are still in the rural areas; migrants who are already in the cities would never agree to participate in the contracted-labor system because it requires that they complete a yearlong contract before being paid most of their wages. However, peasants living in the rural area agree to this contract because contractors

Table 7.1. Employment configurations: Precarious work and precarious existence

	Precarious employment		Precarious existence	
Employment configuration	**Labor market relations**	**Employment relation regulation**	**Migratory patterns**	**Spatial integration**
Mediated	• Organized by contracted labor system • Rural labor market	• Main mechanism is limited mobility • Fines for work violations • Hierarchy on jobsite	Permanent temporariness	Isolated on construction sites creating a "city of walls"
Embedded	• Embedded in and organized by social networks • Rural and urban market	• Main mechanisms emanate from social networks (e.g., enforceable trust and kinship obligation)	Sojourner to settler	Clustered in informal migrant enclaves creating a "city of villages"
Individual	• Spot markets: open and organized street labor markets and/or direct hiring • Urban labor market	• Main mechanism of control is violence/ threat of violence	Floaters	Always visible and vulnerable in public spaces creating a "city of violence"

promise a full year's pay, transportation to the cities, and food and shelter. For these migrants, the contracted-labor system serves a number of purposes: it helps them overcome the barriers to migration, lowers their daily living costs in the city, and minimizes the instability of work and the uncertainty of wages. In this sense, it creates a social safety net that offers them protection in the face of uncertainty. Under this system, contractors hire hundreds and sometimes thousands of men. In most cases, therefore, the social distance between contractor and construction worker is great. Contractors spend most of their time securing jobs, seeking payment, dealing with larger issues, and coordinating their workers across the many jobsites where they are located at any given time. They use team and gang leaders for the day-to-day management. The employment relationships are regulated through mechanisms that are part of the contracted-labor system including limiting mobility, fines for work violations, and reinforcing and exploiting differences among workers.

The most important regulatory mechanism in this employment configuration is limited mobility for workers, which is created by merging spaces for tasks associated with both production and daily reproduction and at the same time spatially separating production and social reproduction. Workers are tied to contractors because they must wait until the end of the year to be paid in full. They are also immobilized physically by their living arrangements; they live in dormitories on jobsites enclosed by walls. These arrangements limit their ability to expand social networks, keeping them "rural" and preventing them from putting down roots in the cities. In sum, this employment configuration relies on, and reproduces, the rural-urban divide and the associated inequality created by this system.

In embedded employment, the main pathway into employment is through social networks, and employment relations are embedded in and regulated by these networks. In contrast to mediated employment, the contractors are much smaller, usually hiring no more than fifty men. They use their diverse social networks to hire workers who are already in the city and those who are still in the countryside, drawing from both the urban and rural labor markets. Workers come into the cities and live in enclaves, or "villages in the city," where their social networks expand and diversify. Dense social networks make it easier for these workers to move from one employer to another, across occupations and even across different industries, creating mobility that contrasts sharply to the immobility of mediated employment. These enclaves and dense social networks act as a safety net for migrants as friends and family help them survive lulls in work. Mechanisms of control evolve out of the spatial relationship between production and social production. In this case, the realm of social reproduction extend into the productive realm as employment relations are regulated by mechanisms evolving from social networks such as enforceable trust, bounded solidarity, and reciprocity. These mechanisms, along with pay-per-job arrangements, drive workers to regulate each other or self-regulate on the jobsite. As a result, employment relations are much less contentious than in mediated employment where the payment system and social organization require low-level managers to induce worker productivity. Finally, these workers tend to "settle" in the cities. However, under China's *hukou* system, they do not have urban citizenship, creating a tenuous existence that is a source of vulnerability.

Finally, in individualized employment, the main pathway into employment is through the street labor markets, and the main mechanism regulating employment relations is violence. These workers are already in the cities, making it an urban labor market. Violence is a primary characteristic of this employment configuration, and it permeates the labor markets, the employment process and the men's lives beyond work. These workers spend much of their time in street labor markets, which are illegal but tolerated. Some are organized street labor markets that have "bosses" who control the market. These markets are volatile, with fights breaking out throughout the day with thugs hired by the bosses, but the police only come when summoned by the bosses. Other migrants choose to frequent the open street markets so they can avoid the labor market bosses, but they face harassment and violence from the local police and the chengguan. Migrants working under individualized employment are so atomized that they do not have alternative protections or mechanisms to counterbalance the highly unequal power relations on the jobsite. As a result, the employment relationship is regulated mainly though violence or the threat of violence. When these workers leave the jobsites and the labor markets, they are still not safe from violence as they occupy public spaces in cities where they face harassment from local residents and the state. These workers are hypermobile, paid a piece rate, and rarely hired for longer-term work, creating conditions similar to unfree labor and eliminating the possibility of social reproduction. Furthermore, they have no access to formal welfare and no informal safety net, as production and daily reproduction are highly precarious as they do not know where, when, or how they will find the next job or next meal.

In sum, the concept of employment configuration highlights labor market mechanisms that connect workers to jobs (contractors/intermediaries, social networks, and spot markets) and regulate employment relations (contracted-labor system, social networks, and violence). This allows us to parse out differences and draw comparisons between formal and informal workers and among different groups of informal workers. These comparisons help explain why migrants end up in certain segments of the labor market, why there is little mobility across employment configurations, why social networks operate differently among different groups of workers, and how employment relations in the informal economy are regulated. It also allows us to compare and contrast the different configurations of production, daily reproduction and social reproduction, along with the ways that workers are (dis)integrated into the cities; illuminating additional dimensions of their precarity and sources of vulnerability.

Comparing Dimensions of Precarity among Informal Workers

Much of the literature on the emergence of precarious work explores multiple dimensions of precarious employment (Vosko, MacDonald, and Campbell 2009; Standing 2011), but with few exceptions (Goldring and Landolt 2011; Kudva 2009), most do not consider precariousness of existence. Among these informal migrant workers in China, the realms of production and social reproduction (and work and home) are merged, albeit in different ways. A full understanding of their precarity requires looking beyond the spatial organization of work to also include an analysis how it is related to the organization of social production (Pearson 2013). This section compares key dimensions of precarity evolving out the spatial organization of production and social production to show how this comprehensive perspective helps challenge some common assumptions regarding precarious workers.

Organization of Production: Income, Job, and Employment Insecurity

Job and income insecurity are central characteristics of precarious employment. Job insecurity refers to the sense that a worker will not be able to remain in a job over time; income instability refers to unstable and inadequate wages (Standing 2011; Vosko, MacDonald, and Campbell 2009). Interestingly, job and income security are not always linked (see table 7.2). As we saw in chapter 3, migrant workers located in mediated employment have relatively high job security but low income security. They stay with the same employer year after year, and the employer provides yearlong contracts, so their employment is relative stable. Because of the practice of withholding wages until the end of the yearlong contract, however, there is a relatively low level of wage security. In contrast, chapter 4 illustrates how workers in embedded employment face low employment security but relatively high wage security. These workers are hired by the job and frequently experience periods without work, but their dense social networks increase their mobility as they hop from job to job across employers and industries, allowing them to maintain fairly stable incomes. Finally, chapter 5 depicts how migrants in individualized employment have both low job and income security. They endure long periods without employment and when they do find jobs, there is a high rate of wage theft (nonpayment).

Precarious work is defined by more than just income and job insecurity. Another important element is what happens to workers when they become unemployed (employment insecurity). For formal workers, employment security is created through access to government unemployment insurance or other social welfare programs. Informal workers lack access to formal employment security but often use alternative mechanisms to create employment security. In mediated employment, the contractors and the contracted-labor system create employment security, and in embedded employment, it is created through dense social networks. Workers can use these alternative mechanisms to access social welfare ranging from housing and food to medical care and loans. In contrast, workers in individualized employment lack access to formal social security and welfare, and there are few alternative mech-

Table 7.2. Job, income, and employment security across employment configurations

Employment configurations	Mediated employment	Embedded Employment	Individualized Employment
Job security	High	Low	Low
Income security	Low	High	Low
Employment security	High–contractors	High–social networks	Low

anisms to minimize the risks of high employment insecurity. As we saw in chapter 5, these men do not even have the option of returning home, so high employment insecurity often forces these workers to move between work, crime, and begging.

In sum, all of these workers perform informal work that provides low wages, long working hours, and difficult and dangerous conditions. In this sense, they share elements of precariousness. However, some elements of precariousness evolve from workers' relationships with employers and the state. They vary across employment configurations and challenge a number of assumptions about precarious and informal work: (1) the idea that income instability is the result of job instability; (2) the idea that informal employment is unregulated; and (3) the belief that informal workers who are denied access to employment security in the form of social welfare "simply return home" if they become unemployed.

The Organization of Social Reproduction and Precarious Existence

This spatial analysis of the organization of work in relation to the organization of social reproduction captures how precarity extends well beyond the workplace into the everyday lives of informal migrant workers. It also focuses attention on the processes and mechanisms that create precariousness for informal workers and opens space to consider the historical contingencies that (re)produce these workers.

In mediated employment, migrant construction workers live and work on jobsites that are surrounded by high walls. Hundreds and sometimes thousands of men are hidden behind those walls, living and working in the city without being part of the city. Temporary businesses and street vendors set up shop outside of the gates to provide goods and services to men who rarely venture far from the jobsite. These migrant workers, despite their numbers, are largely rendered invisible in the cityscapes. They are unregistered yet tolerated by the state. As unregistered residents, they cannot access social welfare, use public services, or be seen in public places. Through this arrangement, cities benefit from "cheap and flexible rural" labor without paying any of the social reproductive costs.

In mediated employment, the organization of production along with the production of space creates what I call "permanently temporary" migrants.

These migrants become permanently temporary because they lose their connections to their hometowns but never manage to develop new roots in the cities. They enter the cities under one-year contracts, and once the work is finished, they return home for two weeks or so before starting a new yearlong contract. The repeated yearlong contracts cause distance to grow between the migrants and their hometowns, friends and families, and land. This distance cannot be shortened by bringing families to the city because dormitory living on jobsites is a central component of mediated employment. These dormitories house only men, and alternative housing is expensive and impractical given that workers move from jobsite to jobsite and from city to city. This means that over time, workers lose their connection not only to rural land but also to their families. Their wives leave them, or they miss the opportunity to marry. This is a bitter irony given that it is often the desire to provide for families (by building new houses and paying for education and health-care costs) that drives these men to migrate in the first place.

In contrast, workers in embedded employment are most likely to develop roots in the cities as they populate the enclaves that are now a notable characteristic of large cities in the Eastern region of China. They bring their families to the cities, create community through new friends and social relationships, send their children to school, find partners, marry and separate, and give birth. The dense social networks in enclaves protect migrants against unemployment and provide other types of informal social welfare that make it possible for them to sustain life in the cities. For example, if a worker is unemployed in the enclaves, their family or hometown friends will help with finances or provide a place to stay. If parents work full-time, friends will help with child care. There are also systems of barter, informal loans and credit that help make life sustainable. These migrants become settlers even though they lack urban citizenship or formal residency.[1] Many settlers have been in the city for a decade or more, and some are second-generation migrants who have grown up primarily in the cities, rarely returning to their hometowns.[2]

However, their existence is full of contradictions. These migrant workers are visible but contained as they tend to stay within their enclaves, workplaces, and tolerated spaces. As enclaves grow and become formalized, they attract increasing attention from local residents and state officials. Because these enclaves operate outside of state regulations, they present a challenge to state legitimacy and control. The state's response takes different forms, including periodic "cleansing" campaigns, demolition and redevelopment, and "spot checks" by urban management officers known for their capriciousness and brutality. These interactions turn migrants' informality into precariousness.

Finally, migrants situated in individualized employment face the most visible, precarious, and marginalized existence. These men usually migrate because their hometown connections are weak or strained; as a result, once they leave home, they rarely return. They enter cities without strong social networks, forcing them to fend for themselves. They lack stable housing, so when they are not working, they often sleep in "hidden public spaces." These migrants are *not* spatially, socially, or politically integrated into the city. Consequently, they are discursively erased as workers and as citizens, more likely to be categorized by the state and local citizens as bums, vagrants, and/or criminals. In public spaces, they are subjected to violence, fines, and harassment. These workers are unable to put down roots in the city or develop strong ties to the enclaves because they must be hypermobile, moving from city to city to find work and survive. The resulting pattern is captured by the term "floaters," which has been (mis)used to describe migrants more generally in China. Perhaps most importantly, social reproduction, daily reproduction (daily survival) and production (work) is highly precarious.

Employment Configurations in and beyond China

Employment configurations can be compared and contrasted across industries, places, and times. For example, mediated employment shares many similarities with other employment arrangements, such as the dormitory labor regime in South China (Pun and Smith 2007) and the South African mining compounds (Burawoy 1985; Higginson 1989; van Onselen 1976). This specific comparison suggests that they are different gendered versions of the same kind of employment configuration. In all three arrangements, the production and daily social reproduction are fused into a single regime that increases both labor flexibility and management control. All three rely on the reproduction of broader social, political, and economic divisions that create and reproduce a segmented labor force; the mining compounds rely on racial and class arrangements; and the Southern China dormitory labor regime and mediated employment among construction workers rely on the rural-urban divide and a gendered division of labor (Lee 1998). Also, in all three cases, workers migrate without families.[3]

However, there are some very important differences between these regimes. For example, the dormitory labor regime in South China facilitates a short-term tenure for migrant workers, and mediated employment among construction workers and the South African mining compounds create long-term flexible labor. In both mediated employment and the South African mining compounds, workers are on yearlong contracts, and withholding wages is common, which creates immobility. In contrast, workers in the dormitory labor regime in South China are much more mobile, and employment relations are regulated by a combination of state intervention, mechanisms that emanate from social networks, and the organization of production (Pun 2005; Lee 1998). There may also be variants of mediated employment among some migrant workers in agricultural work in the United States (Thomas 1992; Wells 1996; Mize 2006), contracted-labor systems in the Middle East (Khan and Harroff-Tavel 2011), and construction workers in other parts of the world (Wells and Jason 2010). Careful comparisons may reveal variants of mediated employment operating in other places or compel scholars to add to the typology of employment configurations.

In terms of embedded employment, it may be most appropriate to compare this employment configuration to arrangements among migrant workers in enclaves in the United States (Portes and Sensenbrenner 1993) and some guest worker arrangements in Europe (Castles 2006). Embedded employment tends to characterize work relations in small private businesses (defined as those with fewer than twelve workers), family businesses, or among the self-employed. This is because small employers and family businesses often rely on social networks to recruit workers, and the work itself is embedded in and regulated by those social networks. However, there are important differences in recruitment, regulation, and the organization of production and social reproduction among small businesses and family businesses.

Finally, on the surface, individualized employment may seem similar to day laborers in the United States, but in reality, these systems are quite different. Both groups use street labor markets to find work, but day laborers in the United States are more embedded in their communities, and in some cases, are more organized, creating worker centers and hiring halls (Fine 2006; Valenzuela 2003). The spatial organization of production and social reproduction is also different and can, in part, be explained by the very different economic and political contexts of the United States and China. Day laborers in China seem more similar to transient and displaced workers during the Great Depression or the Industrial Revolution in the United States, Germany, and England (Crouse 1986; Kocka 1986; Thompson 1964). In all three cases, massive economic transformations produced individualized displaced and transient laborers, effectively eliminating social reproduction for this group. These conditions also challenge daily social reproduction by providing little access to social welfare or charitable assistance to ensure their survival.

We can also compare the labor regimes across cities. For instance, a comparison between Beijing and Guangzhou reveals that there are significant differences in the ways that migrants have been woven into the urban economy and social relations.[4] While all three employment configurations are present, in Beijing the dominant employment configuration is mediated employment, while in Guangzhou, embedded employment prevails. What makes one employment configuration more prevalent than the others? Three factors likely play a role in shaping variation in the labor regimes across these cities.

First is the intensity and type of state regulation of both the labor market and of the migrant population and the political culture that enforces this regulation. In Beijing, the state plays a much more intrusive role in regulating and policing migrant labor, and this could lead to more mediated employment. The number of restrictive regulations and intense enforcement pushes migrants to use an intermediary like the large contractors. In Guangzhou, there is a more relaxed and permissive form of state discipline over residence relations, a kind of diffuse form of *tolerated illegality*, under which embedded employment emerges as the dominant form.[5]

The second factor is the role of foreign direct investment (FDI) in each city. Foreign direct investment represents an important sector in Guangzhou but is minimal and of a different character in Beijing. FDI can impact the migratory regime in two important ways. First, the level and type of FDI changes what is being built from high-rises and mixed used space, large flows of FDI often lead to special economic zones (SEZ) with expansive factories and major infrastructure projects to assure smooth logistics. The nature of FDI is also important as it shapes demand for specific kinds of workforce. In Beijing, the city is connected to the global economy through the service industry, research and development, and technology. In contrast, in Guangdong

FDI is concentrated in the export-oriented manufacturing industry which demands a highly gendered workforce; targeting young women who have not yet married or have not have children.

Finally, a third factor is differences among the migrant population itself. While both cities have significant migrant populations, they differ in total number of migrants, their percentage of the city's population, and the history and development of these migrant flows. Guangzhou is the capital of Guangdong, a province which attracts roughly a third of all migrants in the country, a majority of whom are women. It is also one of four cities which were on Deng's "Southern Tour" in 1992, marking it to be at the forefront of pro-market reform which made it an early destination for long-distance migrants. Beijing is the political capital of the country, and while certainly it has long been the destination of internal migrants, it has also executed a number of large scale purges include after the Tiananmen Square incident, the SARs outbreak, and the 2008 Beijing Olympics.

These cursory comparisons suggest that the concept of employment configuration may provide analytical leverage to understand informal work across different contexts and across the formal-informal divide. The concept brings informal workers—who constitute the majority of workers—back into our analytical framework. It also expands our analysis by fixing our gaze on the relationship between production and social reproduction, nested in a spatial analysis of how these workers are (dis)integrated into the cities where they work, and linked to the creation of precarious and vulnerable workers.

Informal Workers' Protest and Politics under China's Authoritarianism

Informal workers are an important segment of China's emerging precarious working class and crucial to our understanding of labor politics and social change in China.[6] In part, they are easily overlooked because of the tendency to see informal workers as powerless, unorganizable, and impotent. However, these workers do resist exploitation, protest, and organize. This book shows how the issues of contention are shaped by the workers' employment configurations and how their particular forms of struggle are influenced, in part, by the broader context of China's authoritarianism. These structural constraints help us understand why some protesters use "public dramas" while others turn to "protests of disruption" and why they are patterned by persistent, regular acts of resistance on the jobsite punctuated by episodic and dramatic collective action.

In China, as in other countries with repressive governments, informal workers lack institutional mechanisms to collectively express their grievances and seek redress (Bayat 1997; Bienen 1984; Nelson 1979). They are also excluded from formal politics, so they are not subjected to the same kind of bargaining associated with clientelism, populism, or cooptation that are often found in other states (Lourenço-Lindell 2010; Cross 1998a).[7] Furthermore, in places like China, workers who protest or organize using nonlegal channels deal with the threat of violent suppression. In the face of this kind of repression, Scott (1985) suggests peasants (or workers) turn to everyday forms of resistance rather than collective visible protests that challenge those in power. Tilly (2004) shows how the threat of repression in authoritarian regimes forces protests to become clandestine or take place in protected spaces and at authorized gatherings, and Bayat (1997) argues that in these restrictive circumstances, the informal population may "participate in street demonstrations or riots, but only when these methods enjoy a reasonable degree of legitimacy and when they are mobilized by outside leaders" (9). Similarly, Robertson (2010) recognizes that tolerated protests indeed occur in authoritarian regimes, citing China as an example, but he notes that they have great difficulty moving beyond protest to create and maintain social movements and related organizations (22).

The resistance and protests among informal workers that is documented in this book only partially fit these expectations. It takes the form of persistent acts of everyday resistance punctuated by sporadic dramatic eruptions of collective organizing and protests. In this sense, it is more than everyday acts of resistance (Scott 1985) or clandestine protests (Tilly 2004) but, as Robertson (2010) suggests, not as structured as traditional social movement organizing. In some ways, it is a similar form to what Bayat (1997b) calls the "quiet encroachment of the ordinary" (7), which include struggles that oscillate between quiet, individualized prolonged mobilizations and episodic, proactive, highly visible, and audible collective actions, both of which are driven by morality more than rationality.[8]

One way to think about protest forms in China is to construct a spectrum ranging from the most accepted or tolerated forms to the least accepted or tolerated. One end would be represented by protests that use strategies that are within authorized channels, such as filing labor claims in newly established labor tribunals, while the other end of the spectrum is represented by protests strategies and forms that are not tolerated, such as the "protests of disruption" described in this book. In Lee's (2007) study, the migrant workers who engage in "protests against discrimination" based on the new regulatory legal regime range from highly tolerated (filing legal claims) to mostly tolerated. Even when these workers go on strike, which is not prohibited but not a protected right, it hovers around the boundaries of tolerated protest. Likewise, state-owned enterprise workers who participate in "protests of desperation," while sometimes crossing into disruptive strategies, they generally use a number of protest forms, such as petitioning, which are considered to legitimate and have become part of routinized contentious bargaining that stabilizes rather than threatens the regime (Chen 2011). In fact, most public dramas as a form of protests are becoming routinized and share characteristics with the "rightful resistance" described by O'Brien and Li (2006) in their study on resistance in rural China. Rightful resistance, which is a "form of popular contention that operates near the boundary of authorized channels," fits some of the protests among construction workers, especially those using public dramas' to protest against wage arrears. In contrast, construction workers participating in "protests of disruption" are on the far end of the spectrum as they fall outside of authorized channels and are not usually tolerated by the state. These protests are intentionally disruptive, and in many cases, intentionally challenge rather than use the system.

These informal workers utilize public dramas and disruption to gain symbolic leverage, much like the janitors in Chun's (2011) comparative study of marginal workers in the United States and Korea. However, in Chun's study, workers use symbolic struggles as leverage to rebuild their associational power, which derives from collective organizing. In China, because of the political environment, informal construction workers cannot create and sustain formal organizations; instead they adopt a much more fluid form of organizing. Additionally, in China, these public dramas do more than develop symbolic leverage for marginalized workers; they put these workers in the public eye and provide potential protection from capricious state repression, which allows protests to grow and sustain over time and pressures the government to address the injustice. While Chun's (2011) workers "attempt to circumvent existing rules and procedures to reconfigure the relations of power and inequality that underpin flexible work arrangements" (173), informal workers in China are already outside of the existing rules and procedures.

Although informal workers often do not organize formal organizations or participate in sustained protests that we tend to associate with social movements and social change, they should not be underestimated. They are often successful in providing immediate gains for workers, and more important, they sometimes challenge the structural features of the economic system that shapes their vulnerabilities. Protests among informal workers can be more threatening to the state than organizing and protest among formal workers for multiple reasons. First, these workers usually target the state rather than employers. Second, the issues are easily framed as universal and symbolic of larger social struggles, increasing the potential for cross-class support. Third, these protests are public and dramatic, drawing attention and support from a geographically widespread cross-class coalition of people. This strategy also makes it more difficult for the state to use violent repression to crush the protest. Fourth, these protests draw attention to the state's lack of control and question state legitimacy. Finally, even when protests organize to extend across place and time, there are no formal organizing structures, providing the workers with true autonomy. Their lack of sustained formal organization makes it difficult to be co-opted, infiltrated, or crushed by the state.

To conclude, this book maps out some of the characteristics of protests among informal workers but leaves us with the challenge of integrating it into broader theories and understandings of social class, protests, and authoritarianism. Our understanding of labor politics in China would be incomplete without close attention to both the structure of employment configurations and the agency of workers operating within these configurations. This book has shown that informal migrant workers have very different experiences of being in the cities and "becoming workers" in China. The concept of employment configuration helps us understand how larger structures and underlying processes (re)shape their relationships with their hometowns and the countryside, with their employers, and with their host communities. It shows that in China, the process of proletarianization is no longer just a story about moving from fields to factories. So, as these peasants enter into urban informal employment, how do they fit into China's emerging working class and the resulting labor politics?

In trying to answer this question, I refer to Walder's (1984) analysis how the Chinese Communist revolution reshaped China's working class:

> This essay began with the claim that the revolution has created and shaped the Chinese working class that exists today. It will end with an equally bold assertion that the revolution has ushered in the unmaking of the Chinese working class. The process of growing political unity, collective organization, and consciousness of common interests in opposition to other classes—a process described by E. P. Thompson (1966) as the "making" of the English working class early in the nineteenth century, and a process certainly well underway in China by the 1920s—was effectively reversed after 1949. . . . The often-fleeting historical process of growing self-awareness and political self-assertion was ended for the working class-their consciousness was increasingly dictated to them by bureaucrats in a Party claiming to be their historical agent. In this final sense, this "second" Chinese working class is profoundly different from its predecessor. (41–42)

This book ends on a similar note, suggesting that China's economic opening in 1978 ushered in an era of global neoliberal capitalism, once again remaking China's working class. This emerging working class is profoundly different from its predecessor, which was supported by some form of the "iron rice bowl." Instead, the contemporary working class looks much more similar to the pre-1949 structure. At that time, the working class included a small cadre of modern industrial workers and a massive army of precarious workers sustained by migration from rural areas, governed by weak labor protections, and with little social security and few welfare provisions (Perry 1993; Chesneaux 1968). If this description is correct, it challenges us to continue to incorporate a fragmented working class, including a large "precariat" into our theories about labor and labor movements. In this case of China, it also raises the question of whether these informal workers who are outside of the state's emerging legal regulatory framework, and their protests which are beyond the boundaries of the legal regime and beyond the boundaries of tolerated routinized protest, will continue to represent a marginalized and somewhat radical element of labor protests or will they become increasingly destabilizing.

Appendix A

Methods, Sampling, and Access

This book is the product of an ethnographic inquiry into the lives and work of informal migrant construction workers. My definition of ethnography is a study based on close contact with the everyday life of a group, culture, or phenomenon over an extended period that is done in order to develop understanding and insights about whatever is being studied. There are many kinds of ethnographies and different approaches to both collecting the data and analysis (Wacquant 2002; Wilson and Chaddha 2009). This study has been conducted by using grounded theory, working closely with the empirical data, to compare and contrast theories, and figuring out when and how theories apply to different situations.[1] I use the tools of interpretation and reflection to understand employment and labor relations among these informal workers. I explore the relationships these migrants have with other workers, to employers, to state institutions, and to local citizens in order to understand their lives and work.

Theoretical sampling informed what constituted my "research sites." This is an analytical process in which I compared the data to theories to shape my understanding of the topic and to inform where to turn next for data, a process of constant comparisons between and among workers, jobs, jobsites, mobility, housing, and social networks. In the end, I gathered data from four types of research sites: enclaves, construction jobsites, street labor markets, and governmental and nongovernmental organizations. At all four types of sites, I conducted interviews and combined them with participant observation.

Sampling forced me to recognize that not all jobsites are the same. I started by categorizing the residential and commercial sectors into three types of jobsites. The first includes new residential and commercial buildings, such as new apartment complexes, mini shopping areas, and houses. The second includes renovations and remodeling jobsites along with finishing work on new buildings (flooring, trim and molding, fixtures, and painting). The third type includes large commercial sites such as large malls, (golf) resorts, and factory buildings. I then divide the research sites by geographical location (see appendix B).[2] Once I had mapped out the different types of jobsites, I conducted purposeful sampling to make sure that I spent time on different types of jobsites across each of the cities in which I conducted my research.

One of the most common questions that people ask me is, How did you manage to get access to these workers and managers? The process of choosing research sites and then choosing who to interview from those sites, is a biased sampling process. In this case, it was determined by the issue of access. Different sites had different issues when it came to getting access, calling for a wide range of strategies including a snowballing technique, using social networks, and purposeful sampling.[3]

Renovation and repair jobsites were the easiest to access. In some cases these workers and I lived in the same migrant enclave; in other cases, workers would call me and ask to meet. Sometimes I would just stop at a restaurant or building where renovation work was being done and talk to workers. It was also fairly easy to talk with day laborers once I found out where the street markets were located. However, new residential and commercial building jobsites were surrounded by walls and had guarded gates, which presented serious challenges.[4] I used three different strategies to gain access: through managers, making friends with the gatekeepers, and using social networks and a snowballing technique.

Access through Managers

In China, many construction sites are hidden behind tall solid walls with guarded gates. While most pedestrians walk past these walls without giving them a second thought, I slowly meandered by, lingering near the gate as I peered in from afar. Eventually I learned that there are a number of gatekeepers on the construction sites who can grant access to some extent or another. The best access is granted by higher-level management, either the highest level of labor contractor or the site manager. I had been introduced through friends to a few site managers and labor contractors who brought me back to their jobsites, let me interview them, introduced me to other managers on the site, and allowed me to talk with workers. Some managers introduced me to the guards and told them that I was allowed to come and go as I wanted. Others told the guards to give them a call when I came, and they would meet me. High-level labor contractors actually offered the best access because they provided access to both management and workers. Site managers could give me access to other mangers and labor contractors, but it was up to me to gain enough trust of labor contractors so that they would allow me to hang out and talk with their workers. I did gain the trust of contractors and spent many hours talking to workers across different jobsites. Also, eventually I convinced one contractor to let me work on his jobsite. This unimpeded daily interaction was invaluable as it provided me with firsthand experience of this kind of work. Once I worked for one contractor, he helped me set up another work stint under a different contractor, and then eventually one more in another city.

Access through Gatekeepers

However, entry to the jobsite through the management, regardless if it was the site management or the subcontractors, was still entry granted by a boss. This impacts how workers interacted with me and limited their openness. I found two ways to overcome this problem: (1) gaining access through the literal gatekeepers and (2) through actually working on jobsites. For example, one day I was walking down a main street in Beijing and turned onto a new dirt lane passing by some small makeshift restaurant stalls. At the end was a gate that was one of two openings into the world behind a nine-foot-tall blue wall that went on for at least two city blocks. The guard smiled when he saw me, obviously bored. We exchanged greetings, but when he pulled out a cigarette, I knew he wasn't ready for me to leave quite yet. I obliged him since he was the gatekeeper.

This jobsite was not far from where I lived. Every day or two, I would stop by to talk with the guards. There were usually one or two guards, older men, who sat on stools by the gates covering the same shift five days a week. We would sit, smoke, sometimes drink, and talk. They were not originally from Beijing but had joined the People's Liberation Army, and eventually their unit was converted into a construction company in Beijing, at which time they were given a city *hukou* and relocated.[5] They lived in the same "communist-style housing" as I did in the next complex over, but their housing was owned by their employer and was offered as a subsidized benefit of their job. I told them I was researching the construction industry and construction workers in China. They took on the task of educating me. During my visits, once we got past the small talk and formalities, I would ask questions, and they would oblige me with detailed answers. I always thanked them for their wisdom and kindness. I joined them for dinner on their days off and was greeted by their ten-year-old son and eight-year-old daughter, who were instructed to show off their English skills. At the gate, workers would sometimes sit and join us. Eventually I got to know the workers and was allowed to go onto the jobsite to see the buildings and the dorms. Over time my visits turned into a quick chat with the guards and longer visits with workers in the dorms. The managers on this jobsite eventually knew of my visits but didn't bother me, instead looking the other way.[6] Befriending the guards was one method of gaining entry onto the jobsite. This method allowed me to avoid contact with the management. However, it gave me only limited access because it required visits in the evenings after work was done.

Snowball Sampling

I also relied on a process known to researchers as snowballing, in which one person introduced me to the next, a technique important for locating managers, contractors, and workers. For example, construction site managers were more than willing to refer me to former classmates involved in the construction industry. Also, there are usually a number of construction managers per jobsite, all of whom move from jobsite to jobsite. This means that within one company the managers tend to know the managers working at other sites, and I found they were often willing to help me make new contacts.

Large contractors were most difficult to meet, making snowballing essential for accessing this group. The large contractors had social networks that connected them all along China's East Coast. The contractors in these networks shared information about jobs, lent money, and exchanged workers.[7] I found that once I had an established a tight relationship with one contractor, I was part of this network, and one contractor would introduce and vouch for me with the next. Finally, snowball sampling with migrant workers was quite easy given the rise of cell phones. I had my business card printed in English and Chinese and included my Chinese cell phone number, my email, and my QQ address,[8] which I passed it out to everyone. I told workers to pass the information along, emphasizing that I was interested in talking to as many construction workers as possible. After four or five months of research, I began to get calls and text messages from workers whom I had not met, but who had gotten my name from friends or relatives. Some workers wanted to meet with me because they wanted to tell me about their grievances and thought that I might be able to help them by either bringing publicity to it and/or increasing pressure for resolution (a misgiving I quickly corrected); others were simply curious, wanting to meet and talk to a foreigner. Finally, some of the workers called simply to participate in the research (or had some other motive of which I was unaware). Cell phones and the Internet have also helped me stay in touch with this mobile population across time and place.

Interviews and Sampling

Once I was on-site, I had to decide whom I would interview. In many cases my approach was to spend some time on a site (a jobsite, in the enclave, or in a street labor market) before doing interviews. I generally interviewed people with whom I had developed a relationship and who were part of a jobsite that I hadn't covered. For example, if I had interviewed scaffolding workers but hadn't interviewed electricians, I would target an electrician. Or, on a jobsite, I may have interviewed someone from Sichuan but I hadn't yet interviewed someone from the second-largest place-based group, Hunan, so I would try to find someone from Hunan to interview. These groupings of subjects on a site and decisions about whom to interview were determined through a feedback process that included collecting data (interviews and observations) and then analyzing that data, then making a list with new selection criteria based on that analysis, more interviews, more analysis and a new list, and so on.

Once on a jobsite, I also used a variety of methods to interact with workers. Sometimes I was passive and stayed on the edge of the activity, just observing; in other cases, I was more active, participating in work and conversations. On other visits I did participant-observation in which I interacted with people as I observed, hanging out in the dorms and playing cards, chatting or watching TV, or spending time with families cooking and eating. In the migrant enclave where my apartment was located, I would hang out with construction workers, people-watching and chatting, playing pool, or eating and drinking. Finally, in some cases, I experienced more immersion living in the enclave and actually working at some jobsites.

Appendix B

List of Construction Sites

	Beijing	Guangzhou	Shanghai
New residential/commercial (apartments)	Dongmen1 Dongmen2 Houbajai 1** Dongsishi Xizhimen* Muxudi*	Huangsha** Zhongkai* Changgang	Pudong* Dongda
Finishing/renovation	Houbajia 2* Fuchengmen Jishuitan*	Gangding Huanshi**	Faqu
Commercial	Beijingbei* Jiangguomen* Qinghua**	Huangsha2	Laocheng*

* Jobsites where I spent the most time and visited regularly

** Jobsites where I worked

Appendix C

List of Interviews

Interviewee categories	**Number of interviews (2004–5)**	**Number of interviews (2009)**	**Number of interviews (2012)**
Workers from street labor markets	5	3	3
Workers from new residential jobsites	25	4	5
Workers from finishing or renovation segments of industry	9	4	3
Government workers/officials	5	3	4
NGOs/lawyers	7	1	0
Management	14	0	0
Labor subcontractors	12	1	1
Migrants not in the construction industry	6	8	7

Notes

1. Building China and the Making of a New Working Class

1. More than 80 percent of the world's 1 billion smokers live in low- and middle-income countries. The number of male smokers in China exceeds the entire population of the United States.

2. The concept "Chinese Dream" came into prominence when Xi Jinping used it on a tour in 2012 and later in speeches articulating China's goals. It is somewhat vague but includes a "great renewal of the Chinese nation," which will be based on better access to education, stable employment, higher incomes, medical and health care, and social security provisions. It includes the idea that the younger generation should grow up healthy, have satisfactory jobs, and live better lives than their parents.

3. This increasing urbanization is linked to economic development because people are leaving agriculture for more productive work and engaging the market economy more fully.

4. These numbers come from China's 2010 census (http://www.geohive.com/cntry/china.aspx). They vary across lists depending on what definition is used; sometimes Chongqing also appears on lists of megacities.

5. There are still a significant number of workers in state-owned enterprises. However, state-owned enterprises generally produce for the domestic market and do not compete

internationally. There are also local workers in private industry jobs, but these tend to be highly educated and highly skilled workers.

6. See Solinger 1999a; and K. D. Roberts 1997. As compared to local citizens, all temporary migrants, whether registered and unregistered, have reduced access to public housing, medical care, schools, and other social goods, public services, and subsidies. In some cases, they manage to gain access to public services by paying extra money beyond what is charged to locals for their children to attend schools or for their family members to receive health care. In other cases, such as subsidized housing and the national retirement system, they remain locked out.

7. The term "informal economy," as used in this study, includes all activity that is remunerated but hidden from the state (in terms of taxes, social welfare, and labor law) but is legal in other respects (Williams and Windeband 1998). This definition excludes all unpaid work, including trade, barter, "mutual aid" work, and some housework. It also excludes illegal activities (paid or unpaid). In other words, this study focuses on a segment of the informal economy that includes all economic activity that is legal and remunerated but conducted outside of state regulation.

8. This definition comports with that of the International Labour Organization (ILO), including workers in both the formal and informal sectors of the economy who work without social and legal protections (Hussmanns 2004). This definition includes the household and criminal sectors, but the underlying mechanisms and processes operating in these sectors are quite different and so justify separate analyses.

9. There are other overrepresented populations in China's informal economy, including laid-off state-owned enterprise workers, women, and older workers.

10. In 1995, construction workers represented 30 to 50 percent of all migrants (Solinger 1999). In 2002, it was estimated that there were 94 million migrant workers, 31.4 million of them in the construction industry (see "Living and Working Conditions of Construction Industry Manual Worker's," China Construction Ministry 2004).

11. Sampling taught me to recognize that not all jobsites are the same. I started by categorizing the residential and commercial sectors into three types of jobsites. The first includes new residential and commercial buildings, such as new apartment complexes, mini–shopping areas, and houses. The second includes renovations and remodeling jobsites, along with finishing work on new buildings (flooring, trim and molding, fixtures, and painting). The third type includes large commercial sites such as large malls, (golf) resorts, and factory buildings. I then divided the research sites by geographical location. Once I had mapped the different types of jobsites, I conducted purposeful sampling to make sure I spent time on different types of jobsites across each of the cities in which I conducted my research.

12. A number of interviews were not completed. Sometimes I conducted an interview that was interrupted by other migrants who made it impossible to finish or in which the interviewee simply ran out of time. Over time, my strategies for choosing the time and place for interviews minimized these problems.

13. This is supplemented by secondary data including documents form organizations, scholarly papers and talks, and survey data.

14. They are often referred to as "3D jobs": dirty, difficult, and dangerous. The original formal/informal comparison and binary come from Hart 1973.

15. Most scholars who have done work on the informal economy point out that the boundaries have always been blurred.

16. See also M. Chen 2009.

17. Additional studies of street vendors include Donovan 2008; and Zlolniski 2006. For additional studies on domestic workers, see Parreñas 2001; and Blofield 2012.

18. http://www.ilo.org/ifpdial/areas-of-work/labourlaw/WCMS_CON_TXT_IFPDIAL_EMPREL_EN/lang—en/index.htm.

19. Gottfried (2013, 32–35) points out in her critique of Harvey (2008) that feminist political economists have broadened the definition of the economy to include both production and social reproduction, the latter encompassing labor activities required for maintaining and improving the health and welfare of families and communities. While many scholars merge social reproduction and daily reproduction, Pearson (2013, 31) breaks down social reproduction into three categories: (1) biological reproduction (giving birth), (2) generational reproduction (child rearing), and (3) daily reproduction (sleeping, eating, etc.). In this book, I use social reproduction to include biological and generational reproduction and then separate out daily reproduction.

20. Pun (2007) argues that this labor regime is not new but is unique and should be distinguished from dormitory labor provisions that we have seen in other places and times. Pun and Smith also argue that it produces a mobile short-term workforce and is quite different from Western paternalism, the total institutions of prereform China, and the managerial familism of Japan, all of which create and rely on a long-term relationship (2007, 30).

21. State policies in the housing market have denied migrant workers access to housing subsidies or public housing, which moves the limited rental market out of their reach.

22. Burawoy (1985) shows how variations in factory regimes shape variation in worker mobilization whereas Lee (2007) links a changing labor regime in China from the socialist social compact to a legal regime to differences in protest struggles among workers in state-owned factories versus those who are migrants working in the export-oriented manufacturing.

23. Evans and Staveteig (2009) provides a comparison to the United Kingdom, which by 1930 had seen manufacturing become the main mode of employment, representing over 30 percent of all workers. In the United States, manufacturing reached only 20 percent of total employment in the mid-twentieth century.

24. It is important to note here that their conception or ideas about citizenship and rights are not necessarily grounded in the newly established legal regime. When these migrants are making claims to a right to a livelihood and rights to a city they are not turning to the law to establish it as a legal claim, rather they are making a moral claim.

25. This could change as the number of informal workers in individualized employment mushroom.

26. Lee (2007) also argues that theories that explain class politics through analyzing material interest, whether they emerge from the systemic nature of capitalism or socialism, do not offer explanatory power in the case of China. Instead, she argues that worker politics derive from contradictory imperative and tensions in the system, not systemic logics.

2. The *Hukou* System, Migration, and the Construction Industry

1. Agricultural and nonagricultural status was originally granted based on the mother's occupation, not location. This means that the urban/rural and the agricultural/nonagricultural *hukou* divide are not completely correlated. However, more recently, *hukou* status can follow either parent and in many places, the agricultural/nonagricultural distinction has been abolished.

2. In 1978, the Household Responsibility System (HRS) was locally adopted in some places, like Anhui. However, it was not until 1981 that it was officially sanctioned by the central government.

3. Under the 1985 "Measures on Application for and Issuance of Temporary Residence Permits," anyone over the age of sixteen who is away from where his or her place of *hukou* registration for more than one month must apply to the local Public Security Bureau (PSB) for a temporary residence permit. Migrants who do not have the permit cannot get a work permit or a business license, and work units and individual employers are barred from hiring any temporary resident who does not have a permit. Temporary residents who fail to register and their employers can face fines.

4. A large body of literature examines the ongoing changes of this important social and economic institution (see K. Chan and Zhang 1999; and Fan 1999).

5. In Chinese, this group is usually referred to as peasant workers (*nongmingong*), which is distinct from employees (*gugong, zhigong*) and from other workers even if they are manual laborers (*gongren, gongzuozhe*).

6. National Bureau of Statistics of China: www.stats.gov.cn/tjfx/fxbg/t20100319_402628281.htm.

7. Those with *hukou* registration are called migrants (*qianyi*); those without *hukou* registration are often referred to as the floating population (*renkouliudong*).

8. These migrants are referred to as *hukou* migrants in the literature.

9. FL. Wang (2005) cites internal police documents showing that in the 1990s, more than half of the migrants in Beijing and Chongqing were not registered or were "missing," meaning they were not registered either at home or their destination.

10. Two very important exceptions are referenced throughout this book: Guang 2001; and Pun and Lu 2010.

11. In 1951–52 the "Three-Anti, Five-Anti" campaigns focused on eliminating: (1) corruption, waste, and excessive bureaucracy; and (2) crimes by capitalists, which included bribery, theft of state assets, cheating in labor, tax evasion, and stealing state secrets.

12. A *danwei* is a work unit that manages a wide range of the employee's life such as children's education, retirement, entertainment, etc.

13. In 1857–58, the industry underwent a reorganization that still affects the structure of construction. At that time, the industry was geographically reorganized into "construction bases." Each base specialized in a specific craft, was located in a geographical area, and assigned labor, equipment, and resources. This system still operates today in a weakened form and impacts the growing private sector of the construction industry (see Lu and Fox 2001).

14. At this time, contract workers were usually migrant workers hired on one-year contracts. After a major labor law reform in 2008, all workers were required to become "contractor workers."

15. In 2004–5, this issue was mentioned in at least six different conversations during my fieldwork.

16. Regulations on construction quality issued by the Ministry of Construction (MOC) Nov 16, 1993; regulations on construction site management issued by MOC on July 9, 1991.

17. A government labor market is basically a government-run employment agency. However, they are usually specialized so there are some government labor markets for IT specialists, some for college graduates more generally, some for manual workers, and some that are set up specifically to recruit for the construction industry.

18. However, the "iron rice bowl" was cracked (or smashed) by policy changes that replaced lifetime employment with labor contracts.

19. Rural migrant workers make up 80 percent of the industry's workers and about 99 percent of the field workers who work on jobsites and build the buildings, roads, bridges, and houses. If you see a construction worker in China, he/she is most likely a migrant worker.

3. Mediated Employment

1. This myth is not true; it is not visible from the moon. It is sometimes visible from low-Earth orbit, but it is not the only manmade structure visible from low-Earth orbit.

2. Bu dao chang cheng fei hao han.

3. The dominant ethnic group is the Han, which constitutes approximately 92 percent of the population. There are fifty-five recognized minority groups in China that make up the other 8 percent of the population.

4. The "contracted-labor" system in the construction industry should not be confused with the relatively new "labor contract" system that now characterizes China's industrial labor relations, which requires that all employees are given labor contracts that detail the conditions of employment. The former is a system that has evolved in the construction industry characterized by all field workers being hired by an intermediary, the labor contractor.

5. Men represent over 95 percent of construction workers. The few women who work in construction tend to work for contractors from the southern provinces of China.

6. This means that they either (1) have been given overtime, which is a privilege because it is an opportunity to earn extra money, or (2) they have not finished their daily assignments, in which case, the extended working hours are a punishment and not counted as overtime.

7. Large formal labor contractors are registered with the government, usually taking the form of labor companies, and informal labor contractors are not registered with the government. The reforms during the 1990s made it difficult for labor contractors to legally register and ended up pushing labor contractors into the informal market.

8. Construction work, especially in the larger cities, is also considered better work than mining or agricultural work so, for many of them, this is not the bottom rung of the ladder.

9. See Du, Park, and Wang 2005.

10. There is variation in (1) the amount and types of upfront costs that workers face across different contractors (and across place), and (2) which costs are covered upfront by the contractor and which are recovered by the contractor. In most cases, the housing is provided by the contractor, but workers are expected to pay for food. Workers can either choose "free" housing but earn less or choose to be charged for housing and earn a little more.

11. The housing is often subpar but is well below market prices, which minimizes cost of living. The average one bedroom apartment rental outside of the city center in Beijing was about three thousand yuan per month in 2012. This is too expensive for migrants. Even housing that is rented by migrants tends to be subpar because they cannot afford urban rents. Most migrants view their housing in the cities as worse than their housing in the countryside (see W. Wu 2004).

12. This is discussed in detail in chapter 6.

13. He points out that to become a labor contractor on a given construction project, he is often expected to provide a portion of the "investment." In other words, when he is hired to provide the labor for a jobsite, he must pay all upfront costs for that labor, and he will not be compensated until the job is done. The contracting arrangement is a way for the contractor to share this risk with his workers.

14. In part, it is cheaper because workers accept a lower wage in exchange for stable work.

15. The flexibility also allows contractors to minimize the amount of time their workers are idle by moving them across jobsites and cities and sometimes "loaning" them to other contractors.

16. Zhang was responding to a recent government campaign to eliminate labor contractors in the construction industry.

17. The walls and guards also serve other purposes, such as minimizing pilfering of materials and controlling the "fees and fines" that might be issued by local officials and enforcement officers.

18. On this jobsite, the workers live, work, eat, and sleep on the jobsite, and they are forbidden to leave without permission. In some cases, workers are housed off-site but contractors usually provide the housing and transportation to the jobsite. In both cases, contractors limit workers' mobility, demanding that they request permission to leave the jobsite or housing area.

19. A gang leader usually supervises a few work teams, each consisting of from five to six people. The gang leaders are in the middle of the hierarchy of "managers" under a labor contractor.

20. In mediated employment, more than one-fourth of the workers had been working for their current contractor for more than five years, and some of them had been with their contractors for more than ten years.

21. Most workers use the post office to send their money home. They send money via the state-run version of Western Union, wiring transfers back to their villages and towns. This is the cheapest and most reliable method for transferring funds.

22. Money, in the form of wages, is not a form of control in mediated employment. The wage system under mediated employment may seem like it is designed to control workers because contractors could use the threat of nonpayment to regulate workers' behavior. However, mangers and contractors never threaten nonpayment of wages because workers will only work if they believe they will be paid at the end of the year. Therefore, threats of nonpayment were not an effective tool for controlling workers on a day-to-day basis.

23. The infractions they listed included fighting, wasting materials, breaking equipment, health and safety violations (injuries), and leaving the jobsite.

24. Houbajia Fieldnotes (March 17, 2005). "Health and safety violations" are any situation in which someone gets hurt and is caught and fined (or worse).

25. As a result, in Beijing, there is a high probability that workers who mix cement or dig ditches or carrying materials are from Henan or Hunan or even Gansu. Most electricians or plumbers are from Sichuan or Jiangsu. Steelworkers are often from Shandong. However, my sample is small, so I am not certain how consistently this holds true throughout the whole industry in Beijing. During my research in Beijing, I never once met someone from Henan working as an electrician, plumber, or glazier on a contracted-labor jobsite.

26. There were common "cultural" stereotypes about workers from different places. For example, contractors and managers claimed that workers from the North were hardy and strong, and workers from the South were considered highly skilled but lazy.

27. Although contractors claimed that they separated the workers due to cultural and linguistic differences, I believe that they realized that mixing the workers might result in them overcoming their differences and acting in unison. However, although workers realized that they were divided and that this caused problems, no contractor admitted to me that divisions among workers worked to their advantage.

28. Later, some of the workers from Henan suggested that the fight included not only workers from this jobsite but also other Henan workers from another nearby jobsite.

29. In Chinese, the terms are *xiaogong* and *shifu*. Unskilled electricians are actually helpers who train under electricians while performing unskilled or lower skilled tasks.

30. In part, this correlation can be explained by historical tradition. Various towns and cities have been historically designated as "labor bases" or "craft cradles" in which the government promoted development of specific trades and skills.

31. Large jobsites had cooks who cooked two different meals; one for the workers and one for managers. The meals for managers had more variety, more meat, and fewer additives such as MSG, which was used heavily in the food for workers to make them feel full with less food. Workers knew that managers had better food and cherished invitations to join the managers. These rare invitations were extended to small groups of workers.

4. Embedded Employment

1. This is why embedded employment is most similar to what scholars describe when they study migrant enclaves and migrants in the informal economy in the West.

2. Migrant enclaves existed prior to Mao's rule. See also Honig 1992; and Rowe 1984. Bryna Goodman, *Native Place, City and Nation: regional Networks and Identities in Shanghai, 1853–1937* (Berkeley: University of California Press).

3. The government planned to spend 1.5 billion yuan (US$181 million) "renovating" these sites before the Olympics. Another word for enclave is *feidi*.

4. The "villages in the city" can be migrant enclaves or be made up of locals.

5. The estimation comes from the National Bureau of Statistics of People's Republic of China (Zhōnghuá rénmín gònghéguó guójiā tǒngjì jú); and "China's Migrant Workers: No Place to Call Home," *Economist*, June 7, 2007.

6. The majority of the migrants are from Henan, estimated to be 60–70 percent by the local public security station.

7. Some also included Qinghe. Bajiacun can be loosely translated at "Eight family boroughs" which is divided into two sections, the Front and Back (Qián bā jiā and Hòu bā jiā) which are bounded by Qīnghé (North), Xiǎoyuè hé (East), Yuánmíngyuán (West), and Qīnghuá yuan (South).

8. See Beja et al. 1999.

9. Many of the hair salons are fronts for prostitution. In this neighborhood, there was a weak attempt to put up a front that consisted of a sign that said "salon" and a few salon chairs inside. But these establishments did not bother with sinks, hair supplies, or other items that might make the front believable. The city is well aware of this practice and attempts to regulate "salons" through measures such as the requirement that they close by 9:00 p.m.

10. Both the "one-story" housing and the communist era housing are actually owned by locals but usually rented out to migrants.

11. Many of the cars have license plates from other areas that do not allow them to drive in downtown Beijing.

12. There was only one younger Beijinger living in our complex, and he moved in a few months before I left. His family owned a home in downtown Beijing that was taken by the state and sold to investors. They were poorly compensated because the state owns the land and they only owned the apartment. His parents were also laid off from a state-owned enterprise as part of the reforms, forcing them to move into cheaper housing on the outskirts with the migrants. People in our housing complex did not talk to him and were rude when there were forced interactions at our little store. He tried to hang out with us around the store on hot summer nights, but he could usually only stand about an hour of torment before he retreated.

13. I shared an apartment in the older communist apartments with a migrant woman from Guangzhou who worked in a "pink collar" job for a foreign-owned (French) technology company. The process of renting required me to obtain a temporary living permit (also required of the migrants). I had to agree to pay extra money because I wanted to register, which my landlord discouraged, warning me that it would be a hassle. My landlord and I made up a story about her and my mother being friends. We told the government that I was staying with her at the apartment I was to rent (in reality, she was renting it out and living in a new modern high-rise closer to town). We had to make three visits to the local Public Security Bureau (PSB) office and pay a substantial "fee" well above the government allowed limit. We also had to meet with the security person at

the apartment complex and pay him a "fee." Both fees were actually bribes. The process took almost three weeks, requiring numerous documents and terrifying visits to the PSB because my request to live in the enclave was unusual for a foreign student.

14. See Portes and Sensenbrenner 1993.

15. Clan organizations in China tend to be more developed and established than in most places despite the efforts of the Communist Party to eliminate them (see Whyte 1995).

16. She lived a one-room *pingfangzi* where there was no running water or electricity. The shower in my apartment was the first that she had ever used. During the first use, she inadvertently blocked the drain and flooded the bathroom. However, after a few uses, she was an old pro and loved her showers.

17. Fictive kinship ties have a basis different from kinship bonds (which are based on blood and marriage), but they are not less significant. Fictive kinship ties can be as important as those created by blood, marriage, or adoption.

18. Place is a situational concept that can only be understood in context, explaining why the question, "Where are you from?" yields a number of answers. However, in China, people are more likely to ask, "Where is your hometown?" The former is context-dependent; the latter is anchored to the most significant place-based social networks in China: hometown and provincial.

19. Density is determined by the ratio of total connections to total possible connections (the more connections, the denser the network). The strength of a tie is determined by a combination of the amount of time, emotional intensity, the intimacy and reciprocal nature of the relationship between two people (see Granovetter 1973).

20. Sometimes this common identity matches with provincial boundaries, but sometimes the culture is a subculture within a province, such as Subei identity within Jiangsu province. Sometimes the shared identity straddles two or more provincial/political boundaries as in various minority settlements (Hui people in the West).

21. Most college students study English and find it to be a useful skill. I agreed to help her daughter practice her English.

22. This is similar to many cases in the United States such as Chinatown or Little Italy.

23. For example, most enclave leaders know each other and work together in different capacities, which builds their relationships. In other cases, status-based networks are based on social roles such as migrants who are mothers, or they can be based on having attended the same educational institution.

24. Low-density social networks are social networks with a large ratio of total potential connections to actual connections.

25. Mr. Ho first came to Beijing years ago with four men from his village. They formed a construction team and found a lot of work. He hired four more men from the same province out of the enclave. However, two years later the competition had increased. He had a few jobs in a row that failed to pay or only partially paid, leading to unmanageable debt that forced him to give up and head home. A few years later, he decided to return to Beijing and try again.

26. Over the last two years, they have worked for a construction supply store loading materials, as a sorter in recycling, a deliveryman (coal), a cook, and in a metal shop.

27. Daping has the ability to do a number of tasks on the jobsite, but he is also a master electrician—a skilled job that usually provides fairly steady work. Daping could have gotten a yearlong contract in mediated employment but chose to stay with his uncle.

28. He feels an obligation to help his kin and hometown friends when there is little or no work, but he does not feel the same obligation for the other workers, which lightens his burden.

29. In contrast, workers in mediated employment do not interact with migrants beyond the jobsite, making it difficult to develop new social networks. Even when they do develop a new social network, such as those based on occupations, they tend to completely overlap with their existing social networks (e.g., all of the steelworkers in a work group are likely to be from the same hometown and/or have kinship ties). This makes these networks much less effective in spreading information and locating work.

30. In embedded employment, contractors usually have fewer than fifty men working for them, but the majority of these contractors have fewer than twenty men, so anyone with more than twenty is seen as a large contractor. Larger contractors spend their time developing their *guanxi* to keep the work contracts flowing. They also are part of the leadership of the migrant enclaves and often deal with government officials and local businessmen. Small contractors generally have from five to fifteen men working under them, and unlike larger contractors, these men juggle their time between doing manual work on the jobsite and hustling for work. Below the contractors, multitudes of workers are divided into skilled, unskilled, and grunt workers.

31. When he was younger, he served in the Red Guard, but at some point his division was converted into a construction brigade. The construction brigade eventually sent him back to Henan. Years later, he returned to Beijing with a few workers from his hometown and started working as a contractor.

32. From a distance, I observed that, on jobsites dominated by mediated employment, the workers seemed very slow. Their pace of walking, shoveling, hauling, cutting, and hammering was methodical and sometimes sluggish. At first, I attributed the relatively slow pace of work to exhaustion. However, I learned from working on these jobsites that the pace of work was deliberate and under constant negotiation.

33. This is different than a piece rate in which the boss pays workers by task. For example, three cents per brick laid or ten dollars for digging a ditch.

34. In Chinese they often used the phrase Duō láo duō dé.

35. In Chinese: Shíjiān jiùshì jīnqián.

36. This action may or may not be representative of utility maximizing behavior.

37. Workers worked long hours and at a fast pace even when there were no jobs waiting for them. They did this not to make money but to avoid the appearance that they were shirking.

38. The workers are also spatially segregated as a result of the timing of the production process in construction. For example, the first stage of building is foundational work. Those workers are mostly in mediated employment. Once the foundation is finished, they move to a new jobsite, and then new crews come to do the next stage of construction. The last stage, finishing work, is often done by workers in embedded employment. Their jobsites rarely include workers in mediated employment because they have moved on to

new jobsites. It is in the middle stages of the process that the different employment configurations overlap on jobsites.

39. Actually, it is usually differentiated among skilled, unskilled, and grunt workers.

40. Ma and Xiang 1998; Gua and Shen 2003; Dutton 1998.

41. Term used in He 2003.

42. The *chengguan* (called urban or public security force) are charged with enforcing city laws and management. Their mandate is broad, including laws about the environment, vending, health, and sanitation. They were established in 2001, and they tend to focus on migrant workers rather than locals. In social media and via word of mouth, they have become notorious for their abuses of power.

43. Most of the vegetable vendors packed up their vegetables at the end of the night and stored them in a safe place but left their tables. The fruit vendors had constructed a temporary shack behind the table and lived there through the spring, summer, and fall. Therefore, the tables were there all of the time, leaving no impression that the vendors planned to leave. The police did not force the vendors to stop selling as long as they paid the fine.

44. After the first raid, there was speculation that a migrant boss or leader had angered someone in government, leading to the raids. After another raid a few months later, there was speculation that the security forces were looking for criminals who had assaulted some college women (Zhang, personal interview, February 2, 2005).

45. This change is called, "Rules for Relief and Management of Vagrants and Beggars in the Urban Areas."

46. He claims he was charged more because they know he makes more money. However, he also has a record of jail time. I am not sure whether he has a fake ID to avoid problems caused by his past or if the police knew about his record, which made the price higher.

5. Individual Employment

1. In Chinese, the black labor market is called *hei shi chang*.

2. In individualized employment, employment relations are not regulated by the laws as they are for formal workers; they are not regulated by a contracted-labor system as we saw in mediated employment; nor are they regulated by social relations as they are in embedded employment.

3. Song, one of the regulars, had been the victim of a pickpocket and since then kept everything in his bag, but others kept their identity cards and money on their body rather than in their bags. Either way, they were an easy target for theft, which increased their anxiety and kept them on guard.

4. The men number in the hundreds during peak season, which is right after the New Year celebration. Their number can even climb to around a thousand men.

5. The man turned out to be a cousin of the street labor market boss. The police came up as I was leaving.

6. Without his help, spending time in this kind of street labor market would have been impossible.

7. Some of the men milling around have the luxury to do so because they are in good with the market boss, who will ensure that they get work if an opportunity presents itself. Others are resting but will return later to the crowd by the roadside.

8. The person hiring must pay the fee, which is usually anywhere between five and fifteen yuan (US$0.7 to US$3). Special deals are worked out for those who hire large number of workers, and vans line the park waiting to transport people to work locations.

9. Migrant bosses and potential employers don't refer to directly men, migrants or workers. Instead, they use a number of slang terms, often negotiating over "heads."

10. There is one exception. I found migrant workers in the street labor market who were actually employers. They were migrants who needed to hire workers. They would come into the markets dressed as if they were seeking work, leaving behind cars, cell phones, and other gadgets that would betray their identity as employers. These employers would spend some time in the market, talking to workers and identifying those with potential. Eventually, they would make arrangements to pick up the migrant workers outside of the market. These employers, who were migrants themselves, used this method to evade the market fees and to separate the "good" workers from the "troublemakers."

11. In interviews in 2012 with street market participants, migrants suggested that over time, the average age of those who find work in the labor markets is increasing. In some markets, there is also a growing number of middle-aged women looking for cleaning and care work.

12. Violence between migrant workers is not unique to the (organized) street labor market, but it does occur more frequently compared to other settings.

13. The phrase "working is just a waste of time" is translated from *xiangbanyezhishibaigan* in Chinese.

14. False work is all of the work required to build the temporary structures needed for construction projects such as dorms or scaffolding.

15. DaQiang was hired from the street labor market, which surprised me because in Beijing, larger labor contractors rarely, if ever, go to the street market to find workers. On this jobsite, there were workers in both embedded and individualized employment.

16. I was too tired to keep track of what was owed to me, so I relied on DaQiang to let me know how much I had earned each day. We earned different amounts because I quit earlier than he did. It took all of my strength to do the work, so I wasn't keeping track of the number of dump trucks and buckets.

17. A few migrants used a Chinese phrase, *bīshàngliángshān* to describe this situation.

18. Not everyone is completely reliant on the street labor market for work. A few laid-off workers from the factories come to the market only when they cannot find other work. There are also a few migrants who come only for a few months before returning home to help with agricultural work. In these cases, the street labor market provides supplementary work. However, for the vast majority of migrants in the labor markets, this is their primary labor market and their only source of employment.

19. "Chasing the train home" means that he jumped on the train without tickets. He said that some people showed mercy but most just ignored him.

20. This problem of homelessness has only become visible in the recent period since the economic opening, which led to the rise of contingent and precarious work and the influx of migrant workers who often fill these positions.

21. In 2008, a number of migrants reported in interviews that detention centers, instead of just sending them back home, send them to work off their fines in small private enterprises including brickyards, mines, cement factories, and agricultural enterprises far from the cities. Later, in 2012, migrants still reported that the new social service shelters were used as detention centers where they are forcibly detained and beaten.

6. Protest and Organizing among Informal Workers under Restrictive Regimes

1. This operationalizes Lefebvre's idea that space and power are mutually constitutive and shows how spatial practices produce "spaces of representation," which are the actual lived spaces in the city that generate knowledge and possibilities of new organizing principles and sites of resistance (Lefebvre 1991, 10–11).

2. This could be because the pace of work is contested daily, so they often feel in control of their pace of work. Their main complaints concern the quality of food and housing (standard of life) as well as nonpayment of wages.

3. When the gang leader was out of sight, we did not work. Instead, we leaned against our shovels in a squatting position while wiping the sweat off of our faces and smoking cigarettes. The work resumed when someone signaled that he was coming back. Furthermore, when we were working, our pace of shoveling, carrying, and mixing was slower and more deliberate.

4. Others who worked with Yun also suggested that if they did not concede to the increased work pace and workload, they would not be given a contract next year (Fieldnotes, July 12, 2005). This concern arose only when the job was nearing completion.

5. He used the term "da tie chen re," which means, "strike when the iron is hot."

6. There were four work teams of glaziers, three of which were from Jiangsu province. The fourth team was from Shandong province, and their labor contractor was from Jiangsu. The group of workers from Shandong province believed that they were assigned more work or more difficult and dangerous work than the glaziers from Jiangsu province (Fieldnotes, June, 12, 2005).

7. At this stage in the production process, the pace of work is not an issue of contention but a tool (through slowdowns) to bargain over other issues.

8. Interestingly, other cases also exist of wives and children protesting their fathers' and husbands' unpaid wages. A few additional examples include a case of a woman climbing a tower crane in Ningbo, Zhejiang province, to protest her husband's unpaid wages, and children in Yunnan successfully protesting their fathers' unpaid wages (see http://chinadigitaltimes.net/2012/08/child-protesters/.)

9. Other estimates by NGOs have given numbers that are three times this amount. The *Notice of the General Council on Resolving Payment Delay and Default Problems in the Construction Sector in November 2003* (SCPRC, 2003) doubled this figure.

10. This amount covers only the officially recorded wage arrears. In addition, they may have been able to make this claim because the New Year had just finished, so workers were either paid or dispersed.

11. When asked about nonpayment of wages, at least one-third of the migrants interviewed mentioned this event and what it symbolized.

12. Government sources estimate that back wages in the construction industry represent about 72 percent of all unpaid back wages (wage arrears).

13. This occurs in cases where the judiciary determines that an employer is "maliciously failing to pay wages" to an employee. In other cases, an employer can be charged with a crime when it continues to hold a "substantial amount" of an employee's "wages" in arrears even being ordered by authorities to pay workers. In these cases, employers can be sentenced up to three years imprisonment or detention and/or issued a fine.

14. This program was supposedly implemented in six cities. I visited two of the cities and could not find any workers who participated in the program or even knew of the program. Investigators for Human Rights Watch also could not verify implementation of the program.

15. This was an increase of 7.5 percent (see Ministry of Human Resources and Social Security 2013).

16. The official definition of "mass incident" is very broad, which makes it difficult to find an accurate number.

17. The problem of underfunding development projects not only results in nonpayment of wages for migrant field workers but also often leads builders to abandon half-finished projects, which then scar the urban landscape.

18. In putting together many projects, the contractors have to pay the developer to secure the job (a kickback) and also front all of the costs for bringing labor to jobsite, building dorms, feeding workers, and purchasing equipment and tools.

19. Mou Xinsheng, a member of the Sixteenth CPC Central Committee, is one of the highest-ranking officials who has spoken out about this issue and the government's culpability (see http://news.sohu.com/20120313/n337535125.shtml). Also, two local officials in Beijing in the Commission of Urban Planning and the Commission of Housing and Rural-Urban Development also alluded to the link between local governments and the problem of nonpayment of wages in construction during interviews.

20. While nonpayment of wages is the most contentious issue among informal construction workers in mediated employment, it is much less of a problem in embedded employment. Further, while nonpayment is a problem in individualized employment, the issue is much less contentious than in mediated employment. This can be explained in part by the form of payment under each employment configuration. In mediated employment, workers are paid at the end of the yearlong contract, which means that while they do not have to worry about housing and food, they take on a significant risk of not getting paid. In contrast, in embedded employment, workers are paid per job, and because the social distance between the contractors and workers is small, non-payment of wages is much less of an issue. However, workers in embedded employment face variable periods of unemployment between jobs. As a result, wages averaged over the year are low, and workers struggle to meet basic subsistence needs. The problems associated with unstable employment are acute, as housing and food are not usually provided by contractors. Finally, in individualized employment, workers are paid per piece, and wages are withheld until the job is finished. This makes these workers vulnerable to both nonpayment of wages and produces incomes that do not sustain subsistence. However, unlike workers in mediated employment, they expect that they will not get paid and hedge

their bets accordingly. For example, when negotiating with employers, they often push to have food and shelter provided as part of their compensation.

21. Petitioning is a traditional form of collective action that has been used to target the government or political authorities (see Hung 2013). At the same time, legal appeals are a more recently developed form of protest (see Perry and Selden 2003).

22. They do not resist the pace of work because they are paid per job or at a piece rate, respectively. This means that their pace of work is linked to their pay. Also, nonpayment is less of an issue in embedded employment, and, although widespread among workers in individualized employment, it represents not a year's salary but at most a few days of work.

23. In the villages, social networks and connections are dense and pervasive, but for migrants in individualized employment, they are thin and offer little control or support.

24. Most informal migrant workers are tenants. There are a few rich migrant bosses who do become landlords (Zhang 2001). For more details, see Wang, Lin, and Ning 2013.

25. These structures are erected by collective owners who take advantage of the ambiguous status of the land and work in collusion with local state officials and lax enforcement of development regulations. The housing is actually built by peasants who lived on the land and hold the land development rights. They use the land rights to finance development, and, in many cases, they are not restricted by city administration and planning controls because they are still classified as "rural." They usually build as cheaply as possible, creating a low-cost rental market for migrants who are otherwise excluded from the urban housing markets.

26. There are exceptions (see Zhang 2001; and He 2003).

27. This office in English is called the City Urban Management Bureau, but, in both Chinese and English, people colloquially refer to the officers as the *chengguan*.

28. Some cities, such as Shanghai, Guangzhou, and Nanjing also have City Appearance Administrations (*shirong guanliju*) that have a mandate and jurisdiction that overlaps with the *chengguan*.

29. There have been increased efforts on the part of the state to have informal workers join unions or work with legally oriented NGOs to reach this group of workers that is highly independent of the state. In both cases, the state then uses its power either to co-opt and placate workers in the unions or to crack down on activity that they see as too disruptive (see http://talkingunion.wordpress.com/2012/08/07/new-wave-of-crackdowns-on-chinese-labor-ngos-in-guangdong).

7. Informal Precarious Workers, Protests, and Precarious Authoritarianism

1. According to Piore (1979), enclave economies lead to "settlers" because they offer steady jobs and advancement for first-generation migrants.

2. These rare trips home are more about extended family reunions and fulfilling cultural practices related to ancestors.

3. In the factory system, this is done by hiring younger workers without families. In the contracted-labor system, the housing is only for single men and not offered for families.

4. My original comparison included Shanghai, which is in the middle of the spectrum, making it less useful in generating hypothesis, so I focus on the contrast across Beijing in Guangzhou.

5. This may not have always been the case. A decade earlier, Guangdong province was known for its draconian policies dealing with migrants. Guangdong province also made national news due to a case of a migrant (who was actually a student) who was detained and eventually died in the hands of officials. There were a number of reforms to the local *hukou* laws, along with other laws, in an attempt to change this reputation. However, since 2012 there seems to have been another turn, in which policies dealing with migrant workers are increasingly restrictive.

6. This is suggested by the title of P. Huang's (2009) article "China's Neglected Informal Economy: Reality and Theory." There are some notable exceptions such as Otis's (2011) exploration of gender and service work in China and Hu's (2013) and Gaetano's (2004) studies on domestic workers. However, although these studies explore the rise of service employment in China and the intersections of gender and class in China's emerging working class, they do not engage in a discussion of how this might shape class politics on the macro level.

7. This is not to suggest that populism, co-optation, or clientelism do not operate in China; they do, but in ways quite different from what Cross (1998a) describes in Mexico. Also, while populism and clientelism were strong tools used by local governments during the Maoist era, during the reform period, they have been significantly weakened and lost effectiveness. See Lee and Zhang (2013) for a more detailed account.

8. Bayat (1997, 6) criticizes Scott's (1985) implicit adoption of rational choice theory as the explanation of motivation for everyday forms of resistance.

Appendix A. Methods, Sampling, and Access

1. Grounded theory is very malleable. Some grounded theory practitioners are more aligned with positivism, which focuses on data and dispassionate empiricism (Glaser 1992); others merge grounded theory with constructionism (Charmaz 2006; Bryant 2002).

2. I didn't originally include large public projects like dams, subways, or airports.

3. Purposeful sampling was used when I started to classify jobsites (see Appendix B). It was only done once I had developed this classification system. At that point, I intentionally made sure to seek out sites that fit in each box (for each city).

4. It was possible to gain regular access to special sites such as future Olympic sites or special government projects.

5. In China there is a household registration system known as the *hukou* system. If you want to live in the city, you either have to get a temporary city *hukou* or have your rural (agricultural) *hukou* changed to an urban *hukou*, which is very difficult to do. See chapter 2 for more detail.

6. However, I was not the only unauthorized female visitor. There were female prostitutes who regularly joined the managers in their "recreation room." And there were make shift restaurants and "salons" (i.e., covers for prostitution) that were popping up along the street to service the construction site.

7. In other words, if a contractor had extra workers whom he wasn't using, he would contact his other friends who were contractors and "rent out his workers." Furthermore, on large jobsites there was usually more than one labor contractor, and each contractor usually had employees at more than one jobsite.

8. This is a popular chat system used in China (similar to MSN Chat in the United States).

References

Agarwala, Rina. 2008. "Reshaping the Social Contract: Emerging Relations between the State and Informal Labor in India." *Theory and Society* 37, no. 4:375–408.

———. 2009. "An Economic Sociology of Informal Work: The Case of India." *Research in the Sociology of Work* 18:315–42.

Ai-ju, Shie. 2011. "China Became World's Largest Construction Market in 2010." *Want China Times*, March 4. http://www.wantchinatimes.com/news-print-cnt.aspx?id +20110304000094@cid=1102.

Bayat, Asef. 1997a. "Un-Civil Society: The Politics of the 'Informal People.'" *Third World Quarterly* 18, no. 1:53–72.

———. 1997b. *Street politics: poor people's movements in Iran*. New York: Columbia University Press.

Behar, Ruth. 1996. *The Vulnerable Observer: Anthropology That Breaks Your Heart*. Boston: Beacon.

Beja, Jean Philippe, Michel Bonnin, Feng Xiaoshuang, and Tan Can. 1999. "How Social Strata Come to Be Formed: Social Differentiation among the Migrant Peasants of Henan Village in Peking." *China Perspectives*, no. 23:29–41.

Bhatt, Ela. 1984. "Toward Empowerment." *World Development* 17, no. 7:1059–65.

Bienen, Henry. 1984. "Urbanization and Third World Stability." *World Development* 12, no. 7:661–91.

Blofield, Merike. 2012. *Care Work and Class: Domestic Workers' Struggle for Equal Rights in Latin America*. State College: Pennsylvanian State University Press.

Boxun.com. 2013. "nongmingong tiao gangnan style taoxin" (Migrant Workers Jump Gangnam Style for Pay). *Changjiang Daily*.

Brown, Donald E. 1991. *Human Universals*. New York: McGraw-Hill.

Bryant, Antony. 2002. "Re-Grounding Grounded Theory." *Journal of Information Technology Theory and Application* 4, no. 1:25–42.

Burawoy, Michael. 1985. *The politics of production: Factory regimes under capitalism and socialism*: London: Verso.

Cai, Fang, Yang Du, and Ma Wang. 2003. *The Political Economy of Labor Migration (Laodongli Liudong De Zhengzhi Jingjixue)*. Shanghai: Shanghai SanLian Press.

Cai, Fang, Albert Park, and Yaohui Zhao. 2004. "The Chinese Labor Market." Paper presented at "China's Economic Transition: Origins, Mechanisms, and Consequences," Pittsburgh, November 5–7, 2004.

Cai, Yongshun. 2006. *State and Laid-Off Workers in Reform China: The Silence and Collective Action of the Retrenched*. London: Routledge.

——. 2008. "Social Conflicts and Modes of Action in China." *China Journal* no. 59: 89–109.

Carré, Françoise J. 2000. *Nonstandard Work: The Nature and Challenges of Changing Employment Arrangements*. Ithaca, NY: Cornell University Press.

Castells, Manuel, and Alejandro Portes. 1989. "World Underneath: The Origins, Dynamics, and Effects of the Informal Economy." The Informal Economy: Studies in Advanced and Less Developed Countries, edited by Alejandro Portes, Manuel Castells and Lauren A. Benton, 3–12. Baltimore: Johns Hopkins University Press.

Castles, Stephen. 2006. "Guestworkers in Europe: A Resurrection?" *International Migration Review* 40, no. 4:741–66.

Chan, Anita. 2003. "A 'Race to the Bottom' Globalization and China's Labour Standards." *China Perspectives* 46:41–49.

Chan, Anita, and Kaxton Siu. 2012. "Chinese Migrant Workers: Factors Constraining the Emergence of Class Consciousness." In *Peasants and Workers in the Transformation of Urban China,* edited by Beatriz Carrillo and David Goodman, 79–101. London: Edward Elgar.

Chan, Chris King-Chi, and Ngai Pun. 2009. "The Making of a New Working Class? A Study of Collective Actions of Migrant Workers in South China." *China Quarterly* 198:287–303.

Chan, Kam Wing. 2009. "The Chinese Hukou System at 50." *Eurasian Geography and Economics* 50, no. 2:197–221.

——. 2010. "The Household Registration System and Migrant Labor in China: Notes on a Debate." *Population and Development Review* 36, no. 2:357–64.

——. 2011. "Internal Migration in China: Trends, Geography and Policies." Population Distribution, Urbanization, Internal Migration and Development: An International Perspective. Vienna: United Nations Department of Economic and Social Affairs. 81–109.

Chan, Kam Wing, and Will Buckingham. 2008. "Is China Abolishing the Hukou System?" *China Quarterly*, 195:582–606. doi:10.1017/S0305741008000787.

Chan, Kam Wing, Ta Liu, and Yunyan Yang. 1999. "Hukou and Non-Hukou Migrations in China: Comparisons and Contrasts." *International Journal of Population Geography* 5, no. 6:425.

Chan, Kam Wing, and Li Zhang. 1999. "The Hukou System and Rural-Urban Migration in China: Processes and Changes." *China Quarterly* 160:818–55.

Chao, Kang. 1968. *The Construction Industry in Communist China*. Chicago: Aldine.

Charmaz, Kathy. 2006. *Constructing Grounded Theory: A Practical Guide through Qualitative Analysis*. Pine Forge.

Chen, Feng. 2003. "Industrial Restructuring and Workers' Resistance in China." *Modern China,* no. 29 (2):237–262. doi: 10.1177/0097700402250742.

Chen, Martha Alter. 2009. "The Informal IS Normal." *Development Seminar*. Boston. WIEGO Network Organisation for Economic Co-operation and Development (OECD). doi: http://www.oecd.org/els/42544973.pdf.

Chen, Martha Alter, and Joann Vanek. 2013. "Informal Employment Revisited: Theories, Data & Policies." *Indian Journal of Industrial Relations: A Review of Economic & Social Development* 48, no. 3:390–401.

Chen, Xi. 2011. *Social Protest and Contentious Authoritarianism in China*. Cambridge: Cambridge University Press.

Chen, Yuan. 2012. "Yin Weimin: Basic Wages of Migrant Workers Reached a Final Stage of Non-Payment." *Xin Hua News*, March 7.

Cheng, Tiejun, and Mark Selden. 1994. "The Origins and Social Consequences of China's Hukou System." *China Quarterly* 139, no. 1:644–68.

Chesneaux, Jean. 1968. *The Chinese Labor Movement, 1919–1927*. Stanford, CA: Stanford University Press.

China Construction Ministry. 2004. *Living and Working Conditions of Construction Industry Manual Worker's*. Beijing.

China Daily. 2005. "Beijing to Renovate 'Villages within Cities.'" *China Daily*. March 9, 2005.

China State Council. 2006. *China Migrant Worker Investigation and Research Report (zhongguo nongmingong diaoyan baoguo)*. Beijing: China State Council, 365.

China Times. 2004. "Default on Migrant Workers Pay Comes to End." *China Times*. January 17, 2004.

Chinguno, Crispen. 2010. "Trade Unions and Workers in the Periphery: Forging New Forms of Solidarity?" *Journal of Workplace Rights* 15, no. 3/4:367–86.

Cho, Mun Young. 2013. *The Specter of "the People": Urban Poverty in Northeast China*. Ithaca, NY: Cornell University Press.

Chun, Jennifer Jihye. 2009. "Legal Liminality: The Gender and Labour Politics of Organising South Korea's Irregular Workforce." *Third World Quarterly* 30, no. 3:535–50.

——. 2011. *Organizing at the Margins: The Symbolic Politics of Labor in South Korea and the United States*. Ithaca, NY: Cornell University Press.

Cooke, Fang Lee. 2008. "Labor Market Regulations and Informal Employment in China: To What Extent Are Workers Protected?" Paper presented at the Third China Task Force Annual Meeting, Manchester, June 25–26.

Cross, John C. 1998a. "Co-optation, Competition, and Resistance State and Street Vendors in Mexico City." *Latin American Perspectives* 25, no. 2:41–61.

——. 1998b. *Informal Politics: Street Vendors and the State in Mexico City*. Stanford, CA: Stanford University Press.

Crouse, Joan M. 1986. *The Homeless Transient in the Great Depression: New York State, 1929–1941*. Albany: State University of New York Press.

Deng, Xiaomei, and Chunyang Wang. 2006. "Analysis of Tested Effects and Future Development of Employer Payment Bond System" (Yèzhǔ zhīfù dānbǎo zhìdù de shìxíng xiàoguǒ jí fāzhǎn qiánjǐng fēnxī——jīyú duì shēnzhèn, xiàmén gōngchéng dānbǎo zhìdù de shìdiǎn diàochá). *Construction Economy* (*Jian zhu jing ji*), vol. 289, 11:5–8.

Donovan, Michael G. 2008. "Informal Cities and the Contestation of Public Space: The Case of Bogotá's Street Vendors, 1988–2003." *Urban Studies* 45, no. 1:29–51.

Du, Yang, Albert Park, and Sangui Wang. 2005. "Migration and Rural Poverty in China." *Journal of Comparative Economics* 33, no. 4:688–709.

Dutton, Michael Robert. 1998. *Streetlife China*. Cambridge Modern China Series. Cambridge: Cambridge University Press.

Economist. 2007. "No Place to Call Home." *Economist*, June 7.

Evans, Peter, and Sarah Staveteig. 2009. "The Changing Structure of Employment in Contemporary China." In *Creating Wealth and Poverty in Post-socialist China*, edited by Deborah Davis and Feng Wang, 69–82. Stanford, CA: Stanford University Press.

Fan, C. Cindy. 1999. "Migration in a Socialist Transitional Economy: Heterogeneity, Socioeconomic and Spatial Characteristics of Migrants in China and Guangdong Province." *International Migration Review* 33, no. 4:954–87.

Feng, Wang. 1997. "The Breakdown of a Great Wall: Recent Changes in the Household Registration System of China." In *Floating Population and Migration in China: The Impact of Economic Reforms*, edited by Thomas Scharping, 149–66. Hamburg: Institut für Asienkunde.

Fernández-Kelly, María Patricia, and Jon Shefner. 2006. *Out of the Shadows: Political Action and the Informal Economy in Latin America*. State College: Pennsylvania State University Press.

Fine, Janice Ruth. 2006. *Worker Centers: Organizing Communities at the Edge of the Dream*. Ithaca, NY: Cornell University Press.

Florence, Eric. 2004. "Migrant Workers in the Pearl River Delta: Between Discursive Inclusion and Exclusion." In *Migration between States and Markets*, edited by Hein Entzinger, Marco Martiniello, and Cathernie Whitol de Weden, 42–63. Aldershot, UK: Ashgate.

Friedman, Edward, Paul G Pickowicz, and Mark Selden. 2007. *Revolution, resistance, and reform in village China*. New Haven: Yale University Press.

Friedman, Eli, and Ching Kwan Lee. 2010. "Remaking the World of Chinese Labour: A 30–Year Retrospective." *British Journal of Industrial Relations* 48, no. 3:507–33.

Frundt, Henry. 1999. "Cross-Border Organizing in the Apparel Industry: Lessons from Central America and the Caribbean." *Labor Studies Journal* 24, no. 1:89–106.

Gaetano, Arianne M. 2013. "Migrant Domestic Workers in Post-Mao Beijing." In *On the move: Women and rural-to-urban migration in contemporary China*, edited by Arianne M. Gaetano and Tamara Jacka, 41–79. New York: Columbia University Press.

Gallagher, Mary E. 2006. "Mobilizing the Law in China: 'Informed Disenchantment' and the Development of Legal Consciousness." *Law & Society Review* 40, no. 4:783–816.

——. 2011. *Contagious Capitalism: Globalization and the Politics of Labor in China.* Princeton: Princeton University Press.

Giles, John, Albert Park, and Fang Cai. 2006. "Reemployment of Dislocated Workers in Urban China: The Roles of Information and Incentives." *Journal of Comparative Economics* 34, no. 3:582–607.

Glaser, Barney G. 1992. *Emergence vs Forcing: Basics of Grounded Theory Analysis.* Mill Valley, CA: Sociology Press.

Goldring, Luin, and Patricia Landolt. 2011. "Caught in the Work-Citizenship Matrix: The Lasting Effects of Precarious Legal Status on Work for Toronto Immigrants." *Globalizations* 8, no. 3:325–41.

Gordon, Michael E., and Lowell Turner. 2000. *Transnational Cooperation among Labor Unions.* Ithaca, NY: Cornell University Press.

Gottfried, Heidi. 2013. *Gender, Work, and Economy: Unpacking the Global Economy.* Cambridge, UK: Polity.

Granovetter, Mark. 1973. "The Strength of Weak Ties." *American Journal of Sociology* (6) 78:1360–80.

Greif, Avner, and Guido Enrico Tabellini. 2012. *The Clan and the City: Sustaining Cooperation in China and Europe.* WP 445, Italy: IGIER.

Gua, Chaolin, and Hianafa Shen. 2003. "Transformation of Urban Socio-Spatial Structure in Social Market Economies: The Case of Beijing." *Habitate International* 27, no. 1:107–22.

Guang, Lei. 2001. "Reconstituting the Rural Urban Divide: Peasant Migration and the Rise of Orderly Migration in Contemporary China." *Journal of Contemporary China* 10, no. 28:471–93.

——. 2005. "Guerrilla Workfare: Migrant Renovators, State Power and Informal Work in Urban China." *Politics and Society* 33, no. 3:481–506.

Gundogan, Naci, and Mustafa Kemal Bicerli. 2009. "Urbanization and Labor Market Informality in Developing Countries." Munich Personal RePEc Archive. http://mpra.ub.uni-muenchen.de/18247/.

Hanser, Amy. 2006. "A Tale of Two Sales Floors: Changing Service Work Regimes in China." In *Working in China: Ethnographies of Labor and Workplace Transformation*, edited by Ching Kwan Lee. London: Routledge.

Harding, Sandra G. 1987. *Feminism and Methodology: Social Science Issues.* Milton Keynes, Buckinghamshire, UK: Open University Press.

Harris, John. R. and Michael P Todaro. 1970. "Migration, Unemployment and Development: A Two-Sector Analysis." *American Economic Review* 60, no. 1:126–142.

Hart, Keith. 1973. "Informal Income Opportunities and Urban Employment in Ghana." *Journal of Modern African Studies* 11, no. 1:61–89.

Harvey, David. 1985. *The Urbanization of Capital.* Oxford: Basil Blackwell.

He, Frank Xin. 2003. "Sporadic Law Enforcement Campaigns as a Means of Social Control: A Case Study from a Rural Urban Migrant Enclave in Beijing." *Columbia Journal of Asian Law* 17, no. 1:121–45.

He, Xin, Lungang Wang, and Yang Su. 2013. "Above the Roof, beneath the Law: Perceived Justice behind Disruptive Tactics of Migrant Wage Claimants in China." *Law & Society Review* 47, no. 4:703–38.

Higginson, John. 1989. *A Working Class in the Making: Belgian Colonial Labor Policy, Private Enterprise, and the African Mineworker.* Madison: University of Wisconsin Press.

Hishongwa, Ndeutala Selma. 1992. *The Contract Labour System and Its Effects on Family and Social Life in Namibia: A Historical Perspective.* Windhoek, Namibia: Gamsberg Macmillan.

Hondagneu-Sotelo, Pierrette. 2001. *Doméstica: Immigrant Workers Cleaning and Caring in the Shadows of Affluence.* Berkeley: University of California Press.

Honig, Emily. 1992. *Creating Chinese Ethnicity: Subei People in Shanghai, 1850–1980.* New Haven: Yale University Press.

Hsu, Jennifer. 2012. "Layers of the Urban State: Migrant Organisations and the Chinese State." *Urban Studies* 49, no. 16:3513–30.

Hu, Xinying. 2011. *China's New Underclass: Paid Domestic Labour. Contemporary China Series*, no. 73. London: New York: Routledge.

Huang, Philip C. C. 2009. "China's Neglected Informal Economy: Reality and Theory." *Modern China* 35, no. 35 (4):34.

Huang, Yasheng. 2008. *Capitalism with Chinese Characteristics: Entrepreneurship and the State.* Vol. 1. Cambridge: Cambridge University Press.

Huang, Y., Y. Lan, and Y. Bai. 2013. "Development of the Chinese Construction Industry after the Cultural Revolution: Administration Framework, Economic Growth, and Market Structure." *Journal of Architectural Engineering* 19, no. 1:41–50.

Human Rights Watch. 2008. "One Year of My Blood." New York: Human Rights Watch.

——. 2012. *"Beat Him, Take Everything Away": Abuses by China's Chengguan Para-Police.* New York: Human Rights Watch.

Hung, Ho-fung. 2013. *Protest with Chinese Characteristics: Demonstrations, Riots, and Petitions in the Mid-Qing Dynasty.* New York: Columbia University Press.

Hurst, William. 2004. "Understanding Contentious Collective Action by Chinese Laid-Off Workers: The Importance of Regional Political Economy." *Studies in Comparative International Development* 39, no. 2:94–120.

Hussmanns, Ralf. 2004. "Defining and Measuring Informal Employment." Bureau of Statistics Paper. International Labor Organization, Geneva. http://www.ilo.org/public/english/bureau/stat/download/papers/meas.pdf.

Jhabvala, Renana. 2013. "Informal Workers & the Economy." *Indian Journal of Industrial Relations* 48, no. 3:373–386.

Jimu, IM. 2010. "Self-Organized Informal Workers and Trade Unions Initiatives in Malawi: Organizing the Informal Economy." In *Africa's Informal Workers: Collective Agency, Alliances and Transnational Organizing in Urban Africa,* edited by Ilda Lindell. London: Zed.

Kalleberg, Arne L. 2000. "Nonstandard Employment Relations: Part-Time, Temporary and Contract Work." *Annual Review of Sociology* 26 no. 1:341–65.

Kantor, Paula. 2003. "Women's Empowerment through Home–Based Work: Evidence from India." *Development and Change* 34, no. 3:425–45.

Kapoor, Aditi. 2007. "The SEWA Way: Shaping Another Future for Informal Labour." *Futures* 39, no. 5:554–68.

Khan, Azfar, and Hélène Harroff-Tavel. 2011. "Reforming the Kafala: Challenges and Opportunities in Moving Forward." *Asian and Pacific Migration Journal* 20, no. 3–4:293.

King, Gary, Jennifer Pan, and Margaret E. Roberts. 2013. "How Censorship in China Allows Government Criticism but Silences Collective Expression." *American Political Science Review* 107, no. 2:326–43.

Kocka, Jürgen. 1986. "Problems of Working-Class Formation in Germany: The Early Years, 1800–1875." In *Working-Class Formation: Nineteenth-Century Patterns in Western Europe and the United States*, edited by Ira Katznelson and Aristide R. Zolberg. Princeton: Princeton University Press.

Koopmans, Ruud. 1999. "Political. Opportunity. Structure. Some Splitting to Balance the Lumping." *Sociological Forum* no. 14 (1):93–105. doi:10.1023/a:1021644929537.

Kudva, Neema. 2009. "The Everyday and the Episodic: The Spatial and Political Impacts of Urban Informality." *Environment and Planning* 41, no. 7:1614.

Kumar, Sunil, and Bingqin Li. 2007. "Urban Labor Market Changes and Social Protection for Urban Informal Workers." In *China's Emerging Cities: The Making of New Urbanism,* edited by Fulong Wu. London: Routledge.

Lee, Ching Kwan. 1998. *Gender and the South China Miracle: Two Worlds of Factory Women*. Berkeley: University of California Press.

——. 2007. *Against the Law: Labor Protests in China's Rustbelt and Sunbelt*. Berkeley: University of California Press.

Lee, Ching Kwan, and Yuan Shen. 2011. "The Anti-Solidarity Machine? Labor Nongovernmental Organizations in China." *From Iron Rice Bowl to Informalization: Markets, Workers, and the State in a Changing China*. Ithaca, NY: Cornell University Press.

Lee, Ching Kwan, and Yonghong Zhang. 2013. "The Power of Instability: Unraveling the Microfoundations of Bargained Authoritarianism in China." *American Journal of Sociology* 118, no. 6:1475–508.

Lefebvre, H. (1974). 1991: *The Production of Space*. Trans. D. Nicholson-Smith. Cambridge, Oxford: Blackwell.

Li, Daokui. 2007. "Pay Attention to the Decreasing Labor Income Share of GDP" (Zhòngshì GDP zhōng láodòng shōurù bǐzhòng de xiàjiàng). *New Fortune* (*Xīn Cáifù*), September 21.

Liang, Zai, and Zhongdong Ma. 2004. "China's Floating Population: New Evidence from the 2000 Census." *Population and Development Review* 30 no. 3:467–88.

Lillie, Nathan. 2005. "Union Networks and Global Unionism in Maritime Shipping." *Relations Industrielles/Industrial Relations* 60 no. 1:88–111.

Liu, Mingwei. 2010. "Union Organizing in China: Still a Monolithic Labor Movement?" *Industrial and Labor Relations Review* 64 no. 1:30–52.

Lourenço-Lindell, Ilda. 2010. *Africa's Informal Workers: Collective Agency, Alliances and Transnational Organizing in Urban Africa*. London: Zed; in association with the Nordic Africa Institute; distributed in the United States exclusively by Palgrave Macmillan.

Lu, You-Jie, and Paul W. Fox. 2001. "The Construction Industry in China: Image, Employment Prospects, and Skill Requirements." ILO working Paper, 180:1–50. ISBN: 922112858X. Geneva: International Labour Office.

Ma, J. C. Laurence, and Biao Xiang. 1998. "Native Place, Migration and the Emergence of Peasant Enclaves in Beijing." *China Quarterly*, no. 155:546–81.

Marx, Karl, and Ben Fowkes. 1977. *Capital: A Critique of Political Economy*. New York: Vintage.

Massey, Douglas, and Julie A. Phillips. 1999. "The New Labor Market: Immigrants and Wages after Irca." *Demography* 36, no. 2:233–46.

Mather, Celia. 2012. "*Informal Workers' Organizing*." Women in Informal Employment: Globalizing and Organizing (WIEGO) Research Report. Washington, DC: WIEGO and Solidarity Center.

McDowell, Linda. 1992. "Doing Gender: Feminism, Feminists and Research Methods in Human Geography." *Transactions of the Institute of British Geographers*, 17 no. 4: 399–416.

Medina, Martin. 2008. "The Informal Recycling Sector in Developing Countries: Organizing Waste Pickers to Enhance Their Impact." World Bank Publication, *Gridlines* Oct., 44:1–4. Washington, DC.

Menjivar, Cecilia. 2000. *Fragmented Ties: Salvadoran Immigrant Networks in America*. Berkeley: University of California Press.

Milkman, Ruth. 2011. "Immigrant Workers, Precarious Work, and the US Labor Movement." *Globalizations* 8, no. 3:361–72.

Milkman, Ruth, and Kent Wong. 2000. *Organizing Immigrant Workers*. Ithaca, NY: Cornell University Press.

Ministry of Human Resources and Social Security. 2013. *Strengthening Administrative and Judicial Linkage to Crack down on Wage Crimes* (*Jiāqiáng xíngzhèng sīfǎ liándòng yánlì dǎjí qiàn xīn fànzuì*). Beijing, China: Ministry of Human Resources and Social Security (MOHRSS).

Mize, Ronald L. 2006. "Mexican Contract Workers and the U.S. Capitalist Agricultural Labor Process: The Formative Era, 1942–1964." *Rural Sociology* 71, no. 1:85–107.

Murphy, Rachel. 2002. *How Migrant Labor Is Changing Rural China*. Cambridge: Cambridge University Press.

National Bureau of Statistics of China (NBSC). 2009. *Chinese Statistical Yearbook*. Edited by China Statistics. Beijing: China Statistics Press.

———. 2010. *Chinese Statistical Yearbook*. Edited by China Statistics. Beijing: China Statistics Press.

———. 2012a. *Chinese Statistical Yearbook*. Edited by China Statistics. Beijing: China Statistics Press.

———. 2012b. "Statistical Communiqué of the People's Republic of China on the 2012 National Economic and Social Development." Beijing: China Statistics Press.

Naughton, Barry. 2007. *The Chinese Economy: Transitions and Growth*. Cambridge: MIT Press.

Nee, Victor, Jimy M. Sanders, and Scott Sernau. 1994. "Job Transitions in an Immigrant Metropolis: Ethnic Boundaries and the Mixed Economy." *American Sociological Review* 59 no. 6: 849–72.

Nelson, Joan. 1979. *Access to Power: Politics and the Urban Poor in Developing Countries*. Princeton: Princeton University Press.

O'Brien, Kevin J., and Lianjiang Li. 2006. *Rightful Resistance in Rural China*. Cambridge Studies in Contentious Politics. Cambridge: Cambridge University Press.

Oliver, Pamela E., and Daniel J. Myers. 2003. "Networks, Diffusion, and Cycles of Collective Action." In *Social Movements and Networks: Relational Approaches to Collective Action*, edited by Mario Diani and Doug McAdam, 173–203. Oxford: Oxford University Press.

Otis, Eileen M. 2007. "Beyond the Industrial Paradigm: Market-Embedded Labor and the Gender Organization of Global Service Work in China." *American Sociological Review* 73, no. 1:15–36.

——. 2011. *Markets and Bodies: Women, Service Work, and the Making of Inequality in China*. Stanford, CA: Stanford University Press.

Page, Jeremy. 2011. "China Stamps out Southern Unrest." *Wall Street Journal*, June 15.

Park, Albert, and Fang Cai. 2011. "The Informalization of the Chinese Labor Market." In *From Iron Rice Bowl to Informalization: Markets, Workers, and the State in a Changing China*, 17. Ithaca, NY: Cornell University Press.

Parreñas, Rhacel Salazar. 2001. *Servants of Globalization: Women, Migration and Domestic Work*. Stanford, CA: Stanford University Press.

Pearson, Ruth. 2013. "Gender, Globalisation and the Reproduction of Labour: Bringing the State Back In." In *New frontiers in feminist political economy*, edited by Shirin M Rai and Georgina Waylen, 19–42. London: Routledge.

Peng, Yusheng. 2004. "Kinship Networks and Entrepreneurs in China's Transitional Economy." *American Journal of Sociology* 109, no. 5:1045–74.

Perry, Elizabeth J. 1993. *Shanghai on Strike: The Politics of Chinese Labor*. Stanford, CA: Stanford University Press.

Perry, Elizabeth J. and Mark Selden. 2003. *Chinese Society: Change, Conflict and Resistance*. London: Routledge.

Perry, Guillermo E., William F. Maloney, Omar S. Arias, Pablo Fajnzylber, Andrew D. Mason, and Jaime Saavedra-Chanduvi. 2007. *Informality: Exit and Exclusion*. Washington, DC: International Bank for Reconstruction and Development/World Bank.

Piore, Michael J. 1979. *Birds of Passage: Migrant Labor and Industrial Societies*. Cambridge: Cambridge University Press.

Portes, Alejandro. 1995. "Economic Sociology and the Sociology of Immigration: A Conceptual Overview." In *The Economic Sociology of Immigration,* edited by Portes, 1–41. New York: Russell Sage Foundation.

Portes, Alejandro, Manuel Castells, and Lauren Benton, eds. 1989. *The Informal Economy: Studies in Advanced and Less Developed Countries*. Baltimore: John Hopkins University Press.

Portes, Alejandro, and Julia Sensenbrenner. 1993. "Embeddedness and Immigration: Notes on the Social Determinants of Economic Action." *American Journal of Sociology* 98, no. 6:1320–50.

Pun, Ngai. 2005. *Made in China: Women Factory Workers in a Global Workplace*. Durham, NC: Duke University Press.

———. 2007. "Gendering the Dormitory Labor System: Production, Reproduction, and Migrant Labor in South China." *Feminist Economics* 13, nos. 3–4:239–58.

Pun, Ngai and Huilin Lu. 2010. "A Culture of Violence: The Labor Subcontracting System and Collective Action by Construction Workers in Post-Socialist China." *China Journal* 64:143–58.

Pun, Ngai and Chris Smith. 2007. "Putting transnational labour process in its place: the dormitory labour regime in post-socialist China." *Work, Employment & Society* no. 21 (1):27–45.

Qian, Xiaoying, and Zhao Hui. 2004. "*The Construction Sector in the People's Republic of China Policy Analysis on sectoral development and employment challenges.*" Socio-Economic Technical Paper (SETP) no. 15. Geneva: International Labour Organisation, June (2004).

Roberts, Kenneth M. 2002. "Social Inequalities without Class Cleavages in Latin America's Neoliberal Era." *Studies in Comparative International Development* 36, no. 4:3–33.

Roberts, Kenneth D. 1997. "China's 'Tidal Wave' of Migrant Labor: What Can We Learn from Mexican Undocumented Migration to the United States?" *International Migration Review* 31, no. 2: 249–93.

Robertson, Graeme B. 2010. *The Politics of Protest in Hybrid Regimes: Managing Dissent in Post-Communist Russia*. Cambridge: Cambridge University Press.

Rowe, William T. 1978. "Social Stability and Social Change." In *The Cambridge History of China*, edited by Denis Crispin Twitchett and John King Fairbank, 473–562. Cambridge: Cambridge University Press.

———. 1984. *Hankow: Commerce and Society in a Chinese City, 1796–1889*. Stanford, CA: Stanford University Press.

Sassen, Saskia. 1994. "The Informal Economy: Between New Developments and Old Regulations." *Yale Law Journal* 103 no. 8:2289–304.

Schurman, Susan J, Adrienne E. Eaton, F. Scott Bentley, Mary Evans. Daniel Hawkins, Stephen Juan King, and Sahra Ryklief. 2013. "Trade Union Organizing in the Informal Economy: A review of the literature on organizing in Africa. Asia, Latin America, North America and Western, Central and Eastern Europe." Unpublished Report. New Jersey: Rutgers University.

Scott, James C. 1985. *Weapons of the Weak: Everyday Forms of Peasant Resistance*. New Haven: Yale University Press.

———. 1986. "Everyday Forms of Peasant Resistance." *Journal of Peasant Studies* 13, no. 2:5–35.

Seto, Karen C. Michail Fragkias, Burak Güneralp, and Michael K. Reilly. 2011. "A Meta-Analysis of Global Urban Land Expansion." *PloS one* 6, no. 8: e23777.

Sicular, Terry, Yue Ximing, Björn Gustafsson, and Shi Li. 2010. "How Large Is China's Rural-Urban Income Gap?" In *One Country, Two Societies. Rural-Urban Inequality in Contemporary China*. Massachusetts: Harvard University Press.

Silver, Beverly J. 2003. *Forces of Labor: Workers' Movements and Globalization since 1870*. Cambridge: Cambridge University Press.

Silver, Beverly J., and Lu Zhang. 2009. "China as an Emerging Epicenter of World Labor Unrest." In *China and the Transformation of Global Capitalism*, edited by Ho-fung Hung. Baltimore: Johns Hopkins University Press.

Silver, Marc L. 1986. *Under Construction: Work and Alienation in the Building Trades.* SUNY Series in the Sociology of Work. Albany: State University of New York Press.

Sina.com. 2013. "Migrant Workers Dress as Angry Bird and Other Cartoon Characters on Beijing's Streets in Protest over Pay." *Sina. Finance*, February 1, 2013. http://finance.sina.com.cn/china/20130201/113614477116.shtml.

Smil, Vaclav. 2013. *Making the Modern World: Materials and Dematerialization.* West Sussex, United Kingdom: Wiley & Sons.

Smith, Dorothy E. 1987. *The Everyday World as Problematic: A Feminist Sociology.* Toronto: University of Toronto Press.

Solinger, Dorothy J. 1999. *Contesting Citizenship in Urban China: Peasant Migrants, the State, and the Logic of the Market.* Studies of the East Asian Institute, Columbia University. Berkeley: University of California Press.

——. 1999a. "Citizenship Issues in China's Internal Migration: Insights from Comparisons with Germany and Japan." *Political Science Quarterly* 114, no. 3:455–478.

Standing, Guy. 2011. *The Precariat: The New Dangerous Class.* London; New York: Bloomsbury Academic.

Swider, Sarah. 2006. "Working Women of the World Unite? Labor Organizing and Transnational Gender Solidarity among Domestic Workers in Hong Kong." In *Global Feminism: Transnational Women's Activism, Organizing, and Human Rights,* edited by Ferree, Myra Marx, and Aili Mari Tripp, 110–40. New York: New York Press.

——. 2014. "Reshaping China's Urban Citizenship: Street Vendors, Chengguan and Struggles over the Right to the City." *Critical Sociology.* doi:10.1177/0896920514529676.

Tang, Wenfang, and William L. Parish. 2000. *Chinese Urban Life under Reform: The Changing Social Contract.* New York: Cambridge University Press.

Thomas, Robert J. 1992. *Citizenship, Gender, and Work: Social Organization of Industrial Agriculture.* Berkeley: University of California Press.

Thompson, E. P. 1964. *The Making of the English Working Class.* New York: Pantheon.

Tilly, Charles. 2004. *Contention and Democracy in Europe, 1650–2000.* New York: Cambridge University Press.

Tripp, Aili Mari. 1997. *Changing the Rules: The Politics of Liberalization and the Urban Informal Economy in Tanzania.* New York: Cambridge University Press.

Valenzuela, Abel. 2003. "Day Labor Work." *Annual Review of Sociology* 29, 1:307–33.

van Onselen, Charles. 1976. *Chibaro: African Labour in Southern Rhodesia.* London: Pluto.

Vosko, Leah F., Martha MacDonald, and Iain Campbell. 2009. *Gender and the Contours of Precarious Employment.* Routledge Advances in Feminist Economics Series. London: Routledge.

Wacquant, Loïc. 2002. "Scrutinizing the Street: Poverty, Morality, and the Pitfalls of Urban Ethnography." *American Journal of Sociology* 107, no. 6:1468–532.

Walder, Andrew G. 1984. "The Remaking of the Chinese Working Class, 1949–1981." *Modern China* 10, no. 1:3–48.

Wang, Fei-Ling. 2004. "Reformed Migration Control and New Targeted People: China's Hukou System in the 2000s." *China Quarterly* 177:115–32.

——. 2005. *Organizing through Division and Exclusion: China's Hukou System.* Stanford, CA: Stanford University Press.

Wang, Mingfeng, Xiaoling Lin, and Yuemin Ning. 2014. "Shanghai's Urban Villages: Migrants, temporary residence and urban redevelopment." In *Rural migrants in urban China: enclaves and transient urbanism,* edited by Fulong Wu, Fangzhu Zhang, and Christopher J. Webster, 164–81. London: Routledge, Taylor & Francis Group.

Wang, Ying. 2005. "Research on Chinese Peasant Workers (*Zhongguo Nong Min Da Gong Diao Cha*)." In *China's Social Problems Survey and Analysis* (*Dang Dai Zhongguo She Hui Wen Ti Diao Cha Shu Xi*). Beijing: Central Party School of CPC Press (Zhong gong zhong yang dang xiao chu ban she).

Waterman, Peter. 2004. "Adventures of Emancipatory Labour Strategy as the New Global Movement Challenges International Unionism." *Journal of World-Systems Research* 10, no. 1:217–53.

Wells, Jill, and Arthur Jason. 2010. "Employment Relationships and Organizing Strategies in the Informal Construction Sector." *African Studies Quarterly* vol. 11, issues 2 and 3:107–24.

Wells, Miriam J. 1996. *Strawberry Fields: Politics, Class, and Work in California Agriculture.* Ithaca, NY: Cornell University Press.

Whitson, Risa. 2007. "Hidden Struggles: Spaces of Power and Resistance in Informal Work in Urban Argentina." *Environment and Planning A* 39, no. 12:2916.

Whyte, Martin King. 1995. "The Social Roots of China's Economic Development." *China Quarterly* 144:999–1019. doi:10.1017/S0305741000004707.

Williams, Colin C. 2013. "Out of the Shadows: A Classification of Economies by the Size and Character of Their Informal Sector." *Work, Employment & Society*, November 20, 2013. doi:10.1177/0950017013501951.

Williams, Colin C, and Mark A Lansky. 2013. "Informal Employment in Developed and Developing Economies: Perspectives and Policy Responses." *International Labour Review* 152, no. 3–4:355–80.

Williams, Colin C. and John Round. 2008. "Retheorizing the Nature of Informal Employment Some Lessons from Ukraine." *International Sociology* 23, no. 3:367–88.

Williams, Colin C., and J. Windeband. 1998. *Informal Employment in the Advanced Economies: Implications for Work and Welfare.* London: Routledge.

Wilson, William Julius, and Anmol Chaddha. 2009. "The Role of Theory in Ethnographic Research." *Ethnography* 10, no. 4:549–64.

Wong, Linda, and W. P. Huen. 1998. "Reforming the Household Registration System: A Preliminary Glimpse of the Blue Chop Household Registration System in Shanghai and Shenzhen." *International Migration Review* 32, no. 4:974–94.

Wu, Weiping. 2004. "Sources of Migrant Housing Disadvantage in Urban China." *Environment and Planning* vol 36. no. 7:1285–304.

Wu, Xiaogang. 2005. "Registration Status, Labor Migration, and Socioeconomic Attainment in China's Segmented Labor Markets." Research Report 05–579. Michigan: University of Michigan-Ann Arbor Population Studies Center, Institute for Social Research, 1–26.

Wu, Xiaogang, and Donald Treiman. 2004. "The Household Registration System and Social Stratification in China: 1955–1996." *Demography* 41, no. 2:363.

Xinhuan, News Agency. 2012. Printed Speech given by the Minister of Human Resources and Social Security, Yin Weimin, *"China's current employment situation and social security development."* March 7, 2012. http://news.xinhuanet.com/politics/2012lh/2012-03/07/c_111617797.htm.

Xu, Feng. 2013. "Temporary Work in China." In *Temporary Work, Agencies, and Unfree Labor: Insecurity in the New World of Work*, edited by Judy Fudge and Kendra Strauss, 143–163. London: Routledge.

Yun, Chong. 1956. *My Country's Basic Construction Industry* (*Wo guo di ji ben jian she*). Beijing: Workers Press: Xinhua Bookstore (Gong ren chu ban she: Xin hua shu dian fa xing).

Yusuf, Shahid, and Tony Saich. 2008. *China Urbanizes: Consequences, Strategies, and Policies*. Washington, DC: International Bank for Reconstruction and Development/ World Bank Publications.

Zhang, Li. 2001. *Strangers in the City: Reconfigurations of Space, Power, and Social Networks within China's Floating Population*. Stanford, CA: Stanford University Press.

——. 2012. "Economic Migration and Urban Citizenship in China: The Role of Points Systems." *Population and Development Review* 38, no. 3:503–33.

Zhang, L. Simon Zhao, and J. P. Tian. 2003. "Self Help in Housing and Chengzhongcun in China's Urbanization." *International Journal of Urban and Regional Research* 27, no. 4:912–37.

Zhao, Zhong. 2005. "Migration, Labor Market Flexibility, and Wage Determination in China: A Review." *Developing Economies* 43, no. 2:285–312.

Zlolniski, Christian. 2006. *Janitors, Street Vendors, and Activists: The Lives of Mexican Immigrants in Silicon Valley*. Berkeley: University of California Press.

Index